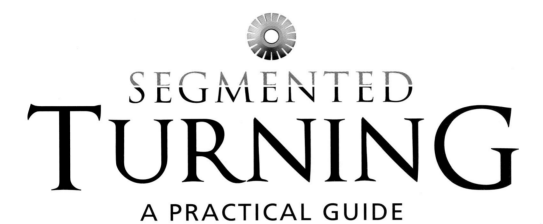

SEGMENTED
TURNING
A PRACTICAL GUIDE

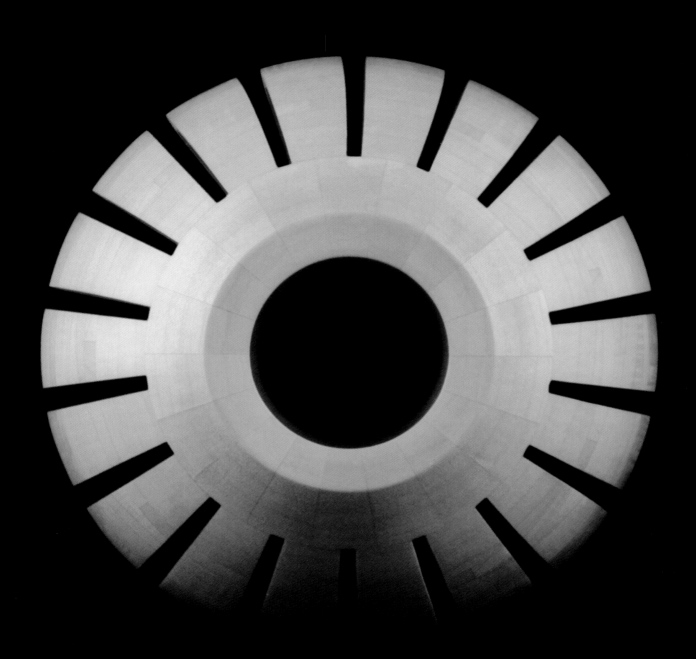

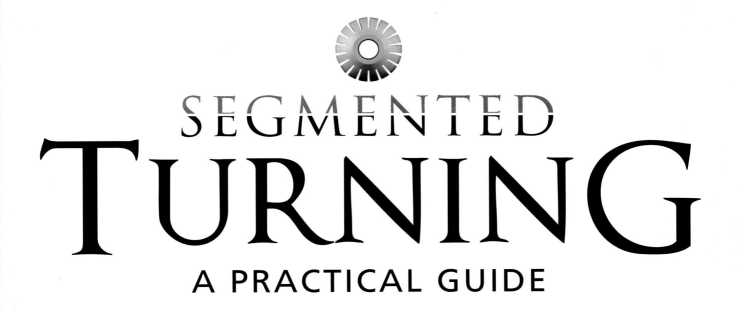

SEGMENTED
TURNING
A PRACTICAL GUIDE

DENNIS KEELING

First published 2012 by
Guild of Master Craftsman Publications Ltd
Castle Place, 166 High Street, Lewes,
East Sussex BN7 1XU

A catalogue record for this book is available from the British Library.

Publisher: Jonathan Bailey
Production Manager: Jim Bulley
Managing Editor: Gerrie Purcell
Senior Project Editor: Dominique Page
Editor: Andrea Hargreaves
Managing Art Editor: Gilda Pacitti
Designer: Rob Janes

Set in Frutiger, Optimus Princeps, and Timeless
Colour origination by GMC Reprographics
Printed and bound by C & C Offset in China

Measurements

When following the projects, use either the metric or imperial measurements: do not mix units, because equivalents are not exact.

Within the cutting lists measurements are expressed as decimal inches only. This is because most segmenters will be using vernier gauges for measurement and sophisticated woodworking machinery that uses decimal scales. Some of the cutting lists are to three decimal places, which is a result of the CAD software used to produce them; however, we recommend using dimensions to one decimal place.

FOREWORD

If you are reading this, there's a good chance that you have an interest in segmented woodturning; in recent years many woodturners have become hooked on it, and those who are looking for new challenges will likely find just what they are looking for in this publication by my friend Dennis Keeling. He has created a wonderful resource that all segmenters and 'want-to-be' segmenters will find very useful.

Segmenting has been around for a very long time, but during the last few decades enthusiasm for this style of woodturning has exploded. In 1973, two English woodturners, Emmett E. Brown and Cyril Brown (no relation) authored *Polychromatic Assembly for Woodturning*. For many years, this was the only widely distributed text on the subject. More recently, however, numerous books, instructional DVDs, and computer software programs have become available and there is now a speciality Internet-based organization devoted strictly to segmented woodturning. Exclusive woodturning symposiums are conducted just for segmenters, and with the efforts of Dennis and others, long gone are the days when turners struggled for years in obscurity as they tried to solve the mysteries of segmented woodturning.

Woodturners have always shared their techniques and methods. Indeed, this is one of the aspects of woodturning that makes it such an attractive hobby – or even profession. I think you will find Dennis's efforts both instructive and inspirational.

Enjoy and have fun.

Malcolm Tibbetts
President, Association of Segmented Woodturners
www.segmentedwoodturners.org

CONTENTS

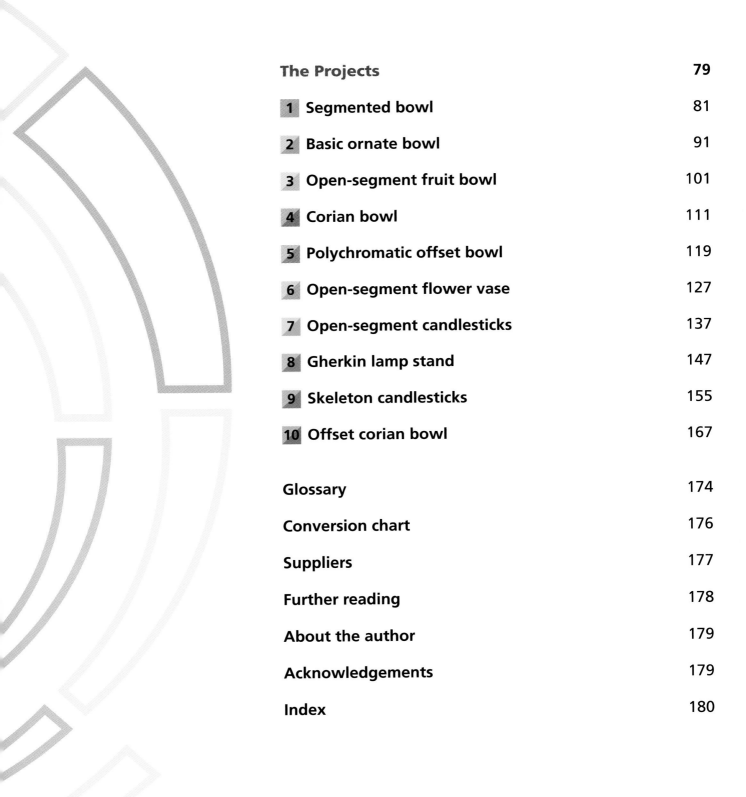

INTRODUCTION

This book contains the segmenting lessons that I have learnt over the years and imparts the wealth of advice given to me by other segmenters, and from which I have greatly benefitted. One of the great attributes of most woodturners, I have found, is their willingness to share information about how they make their unique designs.

I started turning when I was nine years old. Using my father's simple lathe attachment to his electric drill, I cut up broom stays and turned them into spindles. Unfortunately, my grammar school education did not cover woodturning, but years later my wife reintroduced me to the craft when she bought me a lathe for Christmas in 1995.

My early bowls were conventional. However, when I had filled the house with them and had given them to all my friends, I felt it was time to consider a new approach. I knew that segmenting was already becoming established in the USA and fancied having a go. With several planks of hardwood to hand, I wondered if I could glue them together as segments to make a composite bowl. My first segmented bowl was made from beech (*Fagus sylvatica*) using a six-segment design that could be cut at 30°/60° mitres on my mitre block. Soon I was turning Ali-Baba urns, large wine glass shapes, a variety of unusual tubs and other designs.

In 2003, I discovered that Bud Latven, one of the greatest exponents of segmented wood art at the time, was conducting one-week workshops in his studio in the Rocky Mountains of New Mexico, USA, so I invested in a week with him. This was to change my life. During those few days I made a traditional South-West Indian-design bowl, later entering it into the National Woodturning Exhibition at Stoneleigh, England, where it won the Visitors Prize, my first award.

My segmented designs changed quickly after that week; I no longer used chunks of timber as segments – ½in (13mm) segments are normally the largest I employ now. I started to understand how glues should be used and how wood grain should be aligned to prevent the work splitting later, but above all I started to design my work rather than just glue blocks haphazardly together.

A year later, visiting the American Association of Woodturners (AAW) Symposium in Florida, I met Jerry Bennett – famed for his unusual segmented exotic forms – who showed me his SegEasy templates for open-segment construction. I had read articles about open-segment construction, which showed that segments needed to be glued separately using a special jig, which seemed a very time-consuming process. The SegEasy template, however, allows the user to accurately assemble an entire layer for gluing-up all at once, which seems more realistic. He also showed me his Woodturner Studio software package with which to design both open- and closed-segment vessels. I used his CAD software and template to create some very successful pieces. My tall flutes won a prize at the Worshipful Company of Turners of London competition and my Gherkin Lamp Stand won a prize in the International Woodturning Exhibition at the Alexandra Palace, London, competition.

A year ago, while I was demonstrating during a local Open Artist Studios week, a young couple who owned a Corian kitchen worktop manufacturing business asked me if I had thought of using Corian offcuts instead of wood. I saw Corian being utilized for segmented construction by Andy Chen at the AAW Symposium in Albuquerque, New Mexico, in 2009 and thought the idea showed promise. Writing articles for *Woodturning* magazine has steered me into experimenting with other forms of segmenting and laminating, not only with Corian but also with Plexiglas (Perspex) and acrylics.

It's fair to say that in the area of segmenting the old adage 'Everything has already been done' is certainly not true. Segmenters are only limited by their imagination, and when they get together to compare ideas, the atmosphere is electric.

A BRIEF HISTORY OF SEGMENTED TURNING

Using strips of wood to form special shapes is not a new idea. Coopers have been making barrels from staves of wood for centuries. The woodworkers of Tunbridge Wells, England, were making souvenir 'Tunbridgeware' in the early 1840s. This technique uses thin 'sticks' of exotic wood that are glued together to form patterns and pictures. At the same time in Italy, the woodworkers of Sorrento were making similar souvenir objects – the stick technique being quite similar to Tunbridgeware. The Scots were also making souvenir turned items at this time.

Ornate mallet. Tunbridgeware, circa 1860–1880.

The earliest known book on segmented turning was by George Ashdown Audsley in 1911 entitled *The Art of Polychromatic and Decorative Turning*. In 1973, Emmett E. Brown's and Cyril Brown's *Polychromatic Assembly for Woodturning* published by Linden Publishing brought things up to date. These guys were ornamental turners – Emmett from the USA and Cyril from the UK were not related; their collaboration lasted over 10 years, during which time they documented lots of different assembly methods for constructing a variety of segmented objects. This book documents use of segments for utility-ware – now known as Cambridgeware.

Oval plate with stickware and marquetry. Sorrentoware, circa 1880.

Gluing pieces of wood together to make a turned object has become very popular over the last 15 years as a means of creating unusual turned objects. In North America the trend has been towards laminating different-coloured woods together to form interesting patterns. Segmented composites give an excellent base to work from in creating works of art. You will see that the world's leading segmenters use their imagination very creatively.

The basic form of segmenting was cutting planks of wood into segments, staves or laminates and gluing them together to form a composite structure. In this book we will cover basic closed-segment and open-segment construction. We will also examine ways of laminating together different materials, such as plywood, Plexiglass and Corian.

Diamond-shaped sticks, round spindles and parts of complex pictures. Tunbridgeware, circa 1840–1880.

SEGMENTED TURNING'S POPULARITY

Woodturning is such a wide subject, whereas segmented turning brings together a specialist group of woodturners. Segmenters take great pleasure in trying to solve complex mathematical and spatial concepts. Segmented turning is not just about turning skill or design form but also about creating unique objects.

'Tolerance' by Malcolm Tibbetts.
An endless knot ribbon with piercing symbols.

TIME TO CREATE

Rather than produce a simple bowl in an hour and a half, a segmenter will take pride in spending three months in the construction of a piece. After all, segmenters tend to have time to spare. They are not production turners and do not expect to sell their pieces for a price that will cover the manufacturing time.

'Prosperity' by Malcolm Tibbetts contains 8,888 segments.

RECOVERY FROM MISTAKES

One of the great attributes of building segmented objects is that when a mistake occurs, as they inevitably do, the composite can usually be salvaged and reworked. Generally, it is easy to remove a damaged level and replace it with a new one. Obviously some mistakes cannot be rectified, such as cracked wood or joints that have split after the piece has been made. In this book we will focus on problems such as these and how they can be avoided in the future.

Mistakes, such as this, can be rectified. Cut away the damaged area and start again.

Unlimited scope for design

Segmenters are not limited by the size of the lump of timber they are using, but only by their creativity. There are some spectacularly big segmented pieces and also some exceptionally small and complex ones. You only have to look at the Members Gallery on the Segmented Woodturners website at www.segmentedwoodturners.org to see the wide range of designs that have been developed.

When I first started segmented turning I made Ali-Baba urns nearly 48in (1,220mm) high and flutes 30in (760mm) high. Some segmenters have made wooden baths and others have created huge pepper grinders. A wooden composite can be made to any size or design.

Size and design are determined by your imagination.

Economy with materials

When I turned wooden bowls from fresh green wood I was ashamed about the huge volumes of shavings that I generated. Even with bowl savers, cutting out the insides of large bowls into smaller bowls, the pile of shavings was still enormous. Today, my segmented composites are designed for minimum waste. I can use offcuts to great effect. Very little of my timber is wasted. Yes, I do generate chips and sawdust from the machining, but nowhere near as much as I used to create from solid-bowl construction.

Very often I use reclaimed timber. The mahogany (*Meliaceae*) used for the Gherkin Lamp Stand on page 147 was from library shelves that were more than 100 years old. I am often given planks of wood and offcuts from other turners who have no means of using them. My main problem is trying to find a way to use all the planked timber that I have accumulated.

Very little waste is generated from concentric rings.

Main Protagonists

The main protagonists of segmented turning have different approaches to form and design.

Ray Allen

It is widely acknowledged that Ray Allen, from Arizona, was the leading turner specializing in segmenting. His work concentrated on the South-West American-Indian pottery designs. He was the leading player among turners making the multicoloured-segment laminated closed-segment design. Sadly he passed away in 2000.

Ray Allen was famed for his segmented designs influenced by the Native Americans of the South-West USA.

The geometric, repeating patterns on this vessel are typical of Ray Allen's distinctive style.

Bud Latven

Bud Latven moved from basic bowl kits to works of art. He still sells his bowl kits through leading mail-order suppliers in North America and his artwork is continuously shown in the top galleries and museums in New York and Washington.

Today his pieces sell for up to $20,000 and he is possibly the longest established and one of the most successful of the segmented turners. He has inspired turners and artists alike with his unique approach to segmented turning.

'Spiral Impact' by Bud Latven.

Bud Latven's 'Tower'.

MALCOLM TIBBETTS

I watched Malcolm Tibbets demonstrate segmenting and laminating at the AAW Symposium in Orlando, Florida, in 2004. By this time early segmented pieces were starting to show up wood movement and poor construction techniques by the wood splitting or joints separating. Malcolm shared his experiences with the top segmenters around the world and inspired us all to build more durable pieces.

He has written articles, a book, produced several DVDs on the subject, and has become one of the premier segmenters worldwide. By stretching his imagination, he has created an amazing variety of designs and art pieces. He takes great pride in developing incredibly complex pieces that make even the most accomplished segmenters ask the question: 'How did he make that?' Collected around the world, his work is an inspiration to us all. He was one of the founders, and at the time of writing is the President of the Association of Segmented Woodturners. To see more of his work visit www.tahoeturner.com.

'Galactic Journey' by Malcolm Tibbetts. Created from six interlocked pentagon-shaped rings, each large ring is comprised of five outside curves and five inside curves.

'Acceptance' by Malcolm Tibbetts. Ebony and curly maple, 15in (38cm) diameter.

BILL SMITH

Bill is one of the leading exponents of open-segmented turning. I have watched him demonstrate his classic index-wheel gluing jig one segment at a time to create some very small pieces using this precise but flexible technique.

Bill is also one of the founders of the Segmented Woodturners Association. He demonstrates and teaches, and has written the definitive book on open-segmented turning, *Segmented Wood Turning* (A Schiffer Book for Woodworkers), published by Schiffer Publishing. For more information on Bill, go to www.smithart.us.

Bill Smith's 'Tea With A Twist' was designed and constructed for the invitational teapot exhibit at the 2010 AAW symposium. Collection of Sonny Kamm.

Bill Smith's 'Anemones' is made from lack walnut and ash leaf maple. The open-segmented construction then carved onto fluted surfaces.

CURT THEOBALD

Curt Theobold's approach to segmented turning has always been more artistic than that of the typical segmented turner. I watched him demonstrate for the first time in 2004 and have seen him many times since. He is also one of the founders of the Association of Segmented Woodturners.

Both an artist and an instructor, his work is exhibited at some of the largest and most prestigious galleries; Curt also runs segmented-turning workshops in which he demonstrates the processes that he uses to create his unusual pieces. For more information on Curt go to www.curttheobald.com.

Curt Theobald's 'My Mothers'. Curt states: 'This piece was created after the adoption of our daughter from China. My wife is the largest form, the midsized form is our daughter's birth mother and the smallest is, of course, our daughter. The smallest form has both colours (influences of her mothers) in her make up just as my daughter does. The silhouette of the forms is a teardrop, representing the tears of joy, sorrow and uncertainty that all of these people will possess'.

Of 'About the Wizard' Curt says: 'The mystery of the future is exciting. There are many paths set before us that could lead to gold. But often if we look within, what we were so desperately striving for soon reveals itself as folly.'

JERRY BENNETT

I met Jerry Bennett at the Florida AAW Symposium in 2004, where he introduced me to open-segment turning, and I have never looked back. This is also when he showed me his very clever and simple design for a template for open-segment turning (the SegEasy template), which I have featured in several articles. He also introduced me to his woodturning design software, Woodturner Studio, which takes all the maths out of designing and making complex segmented vessels.

Jerry is also a very accomplished segmented tuner in his own right. His pieces are unique and stunning. Driven by fluidity, he certainly pushes the boundaries on how complex segmented structures can be built.

While some of his work is abstract, he tries to represent the human spirit in some way. He believes that Picasso's approach to representation – presenting the essence of an entire subject at once – and the fluidity of Lino Tagliapietra's glass art, have managed to find their way into his work. I certainly agree.

Jerry is careful about not showing how his pieces of art have been constructed. While it is obvious that the pieces are made from wood, how they are made is kept from the admirer. He did, however, finally demonstrate at the Segmenters Symposium in Arrowmont, 2010 how he constructed his unique pieces.

'D' Canter Can't – 'Some decanters can, and some decanters can't!' says Jerry Bennett.

Jerry Bennett called this piece 'Serenade' because, 'When the Philharmonic hits one of those passages that makes the hair stand up on the back of your neck, this is what it feels like.'

DENNIS KEELING

Since building a Mexican bowl with Bud Latven, I have not followed the traditional laminated approach to segmented turning. Instead, I have used the ability to create unusual composites that could never have been created using solid wood alone.

I was inspired by the art of Kenneth Martin whose mobile structures were designed to display intricate interweaving shadow. 'Evolution' is a triple helix made from ash *(Fraxinus spp.)* and brass wire. It revolves slowly with spotlights creating intertwining shadows on the wall.

Today, I try to make functional pieces – candlesticks, bowls, flower vases – which the public is more ready to accept in their homes, than experiment with works of wood art. My recent departure into Corian has been a great success and I am still experimenting with how this medium can be used effectively.

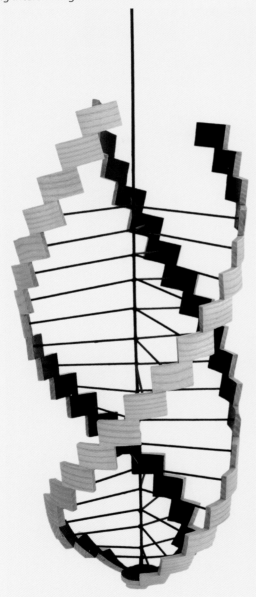

'Evolution' by Dennis Keeling.

An open-segment skeleton lamp stand by Dennis Keeling.

There is still a lot to find out about the use of Corian.

TYPES OF CONSTRUCTION

There are many different types of segmenting. In this book we will attempt five forms.

CONCENTRIC SOLID RINGS

Here, planks of timber or other material such as Corian are cut into rings and glued together.

A simple Corian bowl (see page 111).

CONCENTRIC SEGMENTED RINGS

Here the rings are made up from individual segments. In this book we will refer to the techniques as 'closed-segment construction'.

A segmented bowl for beginners (see page 81).

An ornate segmented bowl (see page 91).

A segmented Corian bowl.

STAVE CONSTRUCTION

In this technique, banana-shaped staves are cut to build up the composite, like a barrel construction but with the staves glued together.

A staved biscuit barrel.

An open-segment stave-construction flower vase (see page 127).

LAMINATIONS

Lamination construction can be many things. In North American parlance, laminations refers to the use of multicoloured segments to create patterns (see my Mexican bowl below, for example). There have been several books written about this specialist pattern technique and so we will not be covering it in detail here.

Historically, however, laminating refers to gluing different woods and materials together. In this book we will cover basic laminating of solid segments (see Basic Ornate Bowl, facing page and on page 91). We will also cover laminating different materials together (see the Polychromatic Offset Bowl below).

OPEN SEGMENTS

In this technique the rings are made from individual segments but with a gap between them. In this book we refer to it as 'open-segment construction'.

A typical Mexican-style bowl.

A polychromatic offset bowl (see page 119).

A pair of skeleton candlesticks (see page 155).

A gherkin-shaped open-segmented lamp stand (see page 147).

EQUIPMENT, TOOLS AND MATERIALS

EQUIPMENT AND TOOLS

The equipment and tools for segmenting are constantly evolving and getting cheaper.

The tools and equipment used for segmenting are slightly different from those required for plain turning. Some of the items are optional, but as one progresses they soon become desirable and eventually essential. That is not to say that you have to have them all to produce a segmented object. Indeed the first project, a simple closed-segment bowl, has been designed as an introduction to segmenting without the need for specialist tools and equipment.

The books written on segmenting even 10 to 15 years ago are not appropriate for today's strict health and safety laws, in particular the use of sledges on circular saws for cutting segments, where the saw blade was unprotected. Today, circular saws have to be used with the saw blade protected and a riving knife fitted. Modern bandsaws and planers also have improved safety guards to ensure that your fingers cannot be damaged accidentally by the blades. Health and safety rules, and many equipment manufacturers, also stipulate the need for dust extraction. This is particularly important for some of the exotic woods, as these can be allergenic and toxic.

There has also been a significant change in the types of tools that are available to the segmenter, for example, the move away from expensive radial-arm saws to inexpensive mitre saws. I replaced my radial-arm saw for an early mitre saw eight years ago but it was not accurate enough for cutting segments so I continued to use the bandsaw. It was only this year, when I upgraded my mitre saw to one of the new thin-blade chop saws, that I realized how they had improved, to deliver accurate and clean cuts. As you can see, then, today's segmenting equipment is quite different to that used by the technique's American pioneers 15 years ago.

Segmenters need a wide range of woodworking machinery.

A solid circular saw with a cast-iron table.

EQUIPMENT

CIRCULAR SAW

Wood used for segmented objects is usually supplied in plank form so that your timber will need to be cut to width. The ideal piece of equipment for cutting long strips of wood to width is a circular saw, now much cheaper thanks to imports from the Far East that come complete with silent induction motors with automatic braking. They all require sophisticated extraction equipment.

Builders use rugged site saws, capable of cutting large roofing timbers, but these do not always have the accuracy of a solid tablesaw designed for workshop use.

A heavy tablesaw with a cast-iron saw carriage and a sliding table gives the repeatable accuracy needed for segmenting. A tablesaw with a 10in (254mm) saw blade gives a depth of cut of about 3⅛in (80mm), which is usually fine for segmenting. A 12in (305mm) blade normally gives a 4in (100mm) depth of cut.

Opt for a tablesaw rather than a site saw.

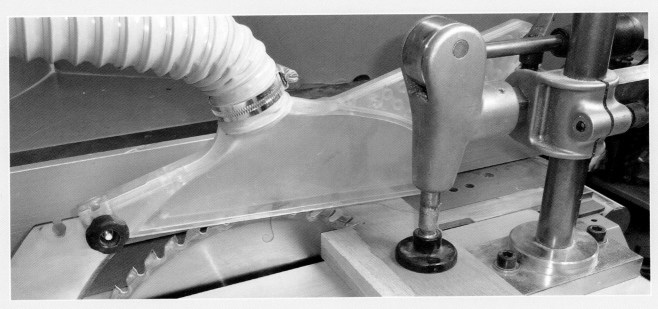

Circular saws can be used for ripping and cross-grain cutting.

Saw blades

Blade technology has also changed considerably. The new thin tungsten-tipped, laser-cut blades offer a totally different approach to cutting with a circular saw. While some of these blades can be expensive, they last considerably longer between sharpening than the old-fashioned blades and can also save a considerable amount of material that would have previously been taken away as sawdust. While these tungsten-tipped blades cannot be sharpened with a file, professional sharpening costs a surprisingly small amount.

The circular saw is mostly used for dimensioning timber. Lengths used for segmenting are cut along the grain of the wood. This is called rip sawing and needs a specialist rip-saw tooth blade. These vary from 12 to 32 teeth.

A different type of blade is used for cross-cutting timber and should not be used for rip sawing. These vary from 36 to 120 teeth. (See picture of cross-grain cutting on previous page.)

General-purpose blades, to enable both cross-cutting and rip sawing, are not as well suited to ripping as a specialist rip-saw blade.

A simple way to check both the suitability of the blade and also its sharpness is to cut a length of wood. It should cut easily without undue pressure and without scorching the timber.

Acrylics and Corian have no grain and can splinter easily, so a special fine-toothed blade for cutting laminates is required for dealing with these materials.

Thin tungsten-tipped, laser-cut blades are dearer but last much longer between sharpening sessions.

Rip-saw side view showing the cut limiter.

Rip-saw blades have between 12 and 32 teeth.

Many teeth with no limiter.

Cross-cut blades vary between 36 and 120 teeth and should not be used for rip sawing.

The teeth have alternating cutting angles.

A laminating blade for cutting Corian and plastics.

A combination machine is practical for a small workshop but changing between modes is time consuming.

The planer is used to flatten the face of the timber.

The thicknesser is used to ensure the thickness is constant.

PLANER THICKNESSER

One of the key requirements for segmenting is flat timber that has a uniform thickness along its length. Pre-planed timber can be used, but sooner or later segmenters will want to plane their own timber to size.

For a small workshop, a combined planer and thicknesser will be suitable. The machine can be set up for either planing or thicknessing modes by moving the table set-up, a time-consuming operation. Segmenters, however, are always moving between planing and thicknessing modes and, to save time, I sold my combination machine and bought a separate planer (also known as a jointer) and thicknesser. I was surprised how cheap the separate units were compared with the combination machine. They are certainly more accurate and time saving, but they do take up more valuable workshop space.

The planer is used to ensure the rough-cut timber is flat (face) and that one edge is at right angles to the face. The wood is then ready for dimensioning on the circular saw. This is the 'face' and 'edge' process that some of us were taught in the woodworking class at school.

The thicknesser is used to bring the timber down to the correct thickness and to ensure that the thickness is uniform along its length. Faces but not edges are machined to their finished dimension using a thicknesser.

Ideally, an 8in (200mm) planer width and a 4in (100mm) thicknesser height are good starting points for segmenters.

BANDSAW

Woodturners find the bandsaw invaluable for cutting wet wood to size. Modern bandsaws vary in size and capability. Some machines still use noisy brush motors whereas the slightly more expensive models are equipped with the quieter induction motors. The throat height (the thickness of timber that can be cut) and the fence width (the width of timber that can be cut) are usually the critical dimensions.

Small bandsaws can cut 4¾in (120mm) height and 9½in (240mm) width, but experienced turners prefer to have bandsaws capable of 12in (305mm) height and 16in (405mm) width cut. For cutting segments on a bandsaw a mitre fence and a rip fence will be required. The mitre fence does not have to be very accurate, as the finished angle will be machined afterwards on the disc sander.

Many types of bandsaw blades are available, offering different widths and tooth patterns. Segmenters are cross cutting wood segments, so a 4–6tpi (teeth per inch) skip form blade is ideal. Since the cut is a straight cut rather than for contour sawing, a wider blade will ensure a cleaner result. Go for, say, ⅜in (10mm) to ⁹⁄₁₆in (15mm).

The thickness of the blade (the kerf) is also important, especially when you are trying to save expensive material when cutting hundreds of segments. Most blades are 0.025in thick, but special bright-steel blades manufactured for the meat and fish industry are only 0.014in thick and cut hardwood easily with less waste.

For cutting acrylics and Corian, ideally a 14tpi regular blade should be used.

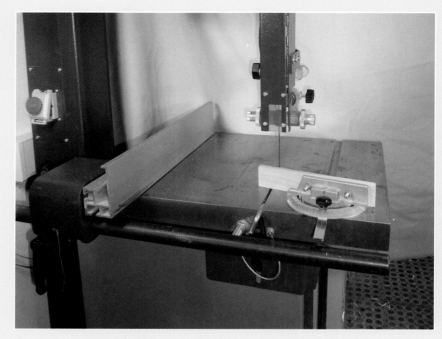

Woodturners need a wide table and a good throat height.

The bandsaw is a safe way of cutting segments.

DISC SANDER

In order to complement the poor sawn edge created by the bandsaw, a disc sander is normally used to tidy up the edge and the mitre angle accurately.

There are various disc-sanding machines available. Some are combination machines with integral belt sanders and others are dedicated disc sanders.

Having tried all sorts, the one I find most accurate and suitable for segmenting is a 12in (305mm) dedicated disc sander.

Since the mitre angle has to be accurately determined – especially for closed-segment work – it may be worth considering purchasing an accurate mitre gauge with pre-set angles. The sanding disks are available from 80 to 200 grit. I prefer 120 grit for cleaning up hardwood segments. Sometimes resinous woods will clog the grain of the sandpaper. This can easily be removed by using a rubber cleaning stick.

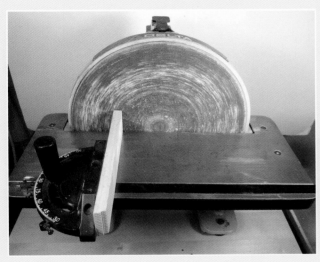

A 12in (305mm) disc sander with a standard mitre gauge.

A sophisticated mitre gauge with pre-set angles.

DRUM SANDER

A 'nice to have' machine for solid segmenting work is a drum sander, which is used to flatten the individual glued-up segment rings prior to gluing up the composite structure. Drum sanders come in various sizes and complexity, varying from the simple single-sided version that I use to more sophisticated closed-sided machines. Segment rings are normally up to 15in (380mm) wide, so the 12–18in (305–460mm) drum sander is ideal, unless you are planning a very wide structure.

The sandpaper roll that winds around the drum comes in various degrees of coarseness, the most suitable for segmenting being 120 grit.

The problem with the single-sided drum sander is setting up the sanding arm to ensure uniform thickness around the ring. This is a made more difficult because it is affected by the depth of cut: a light cut will not affect the setting but a deeper cut will tend to make the ring wedge-shaped. Turning the ring through 45° after sanding, then repeating the last cut, will compensate for any inaccuracy.

Drum sander – ideal for sanding flat segment rings.

MITRE SAW

Manual mitre saws can be used for cutting segments but it is a laborious process – especially as most of the projects in this book have more than 500 segments – but modern technology has improved the electric mitre saw considerably. Motors are quieter, improved bearings provide a more accurate cut and the new thin saw blades cut very cleanly.

Mitre saws come in all shapes and sizes, from simple chop saws to compound sliding carriages, ranging in price from relatively cheap to very expensive; their cost relating to the accuracy and the range of cuts that can be undertaken.

My old mitre saw had a sliding carriage for cutting wide pieces, but with the sliding carriage came inaccuracy. My new chop saw (without any sliding carriage) gives a clean and accurate cut that needs no further finishing.

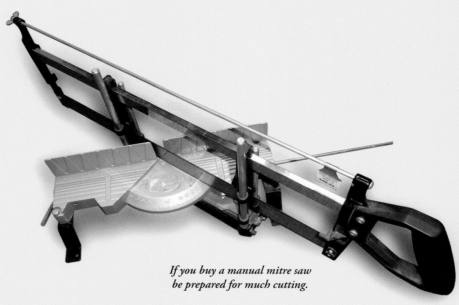

If you buy a manual mitre saw be prepared for much cutting.

Most chop saws come with a standard general-purpose blade. Blades can be upgraded, if required, to more teeth per inch and a thinner kerf. The blade supplied with my chop saw is 10in (255mm) diameter with 48 teeth, which is ideal for cutting hardwood segments. Some segmenters use 96- and 120-tooth blades.

Some segmenters use 96- and 120-tooth blades.

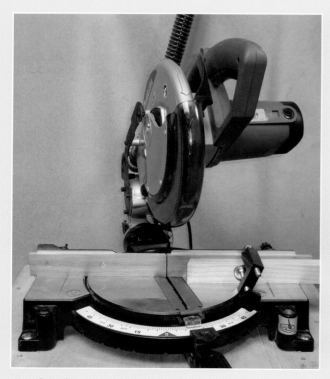

A modern chop saw with thin-kerf blade.

A clean cut without the need for sanding.

LATHE

When it comes to lathe choice segmenting is not so demanding as some specialist applications. The most important requirement is that your machine is a centre lathe rather than a bowl lathe. My previous lathe was a bowl model that could be adapted for between-centres turning, but it was not accurate enough, especially when gluing up the composite. My new lathe is a conventional variable-speed centre lathe, and it works well.

Segmenters tend to use modern chucks for holding their work. When the segment rings are glued to the composite by support pressure from the tailstock, it is important that the centres are accurately aligned, otherwise the joints will move as the structure is revolved on the lathe. When both ends are held between centres this is not a problem as the structure can safely move; it is only a problem when one end is held rigidly by a chuck.

A standard centre lathe with a 24in (610mm) swing.

Most medium-sized wood lathes have high centre swings of 9–12in (230–305mm) to allow wooden pieces to be turned from 18–24in (460–610mm) in diameter. A metalwork lathe and a small pen-turning lathe usually have a much smaller swing of 6in (150mm).

Some wood lathes have a bowl attachment on the side of the lathe bed, but that is of no use for gluing-up segmented composite structures. Choose a lathe that will provide a swing over the lathe bed that is large enough for your biggest projects.

Segmented structures do not require high turning speeds, and a top speed of 1000–1500rpm is fine for most hardwoods, but Corian and acrylics require slower speeds of 500–1000rpm. It is, therefore, a great asset to have a variable-speed lathe with a very slow-speed facility, which is ideal for sanding the face of the composite.

A variable speed control is a must for segmenting.

LATHE EQUIPMENT

Some of the more complex segmented structures require the use of a three-point lathe steady. This device allows for tall pieces of work to be supported while being turned as the structure progresses; they would be too tall to be turned afterwards. Delicate pieces such as the Skeleton Candlesticks on page 155 require support when turning the inside before the candle holder is glued into place.

Some of the Corian structures are off-centre when initially starting to turn; the bowl steady provides a runway to hold the structure safely while the initial cuts are being taken.

There are many different chucks on the market, all with their own unique sets of jaws, which are usually incompatible with each other. It's best to find one chuck manufacturer with a chuck that will enable you to select from a wide range of jaw types and sizes – from dovetail jaws to gripper jaws for spindles from 1–5in (25–125mm) diameter.

The new breed of mega-chucks, offering a wide range of jaw movement, can provide a seamless work-holding range up to 16in (405mm) with large button jaws. Button jaws are ideal for platter and Corian work where wide, flat pieces are being turned. They are also a simple way of undertaking off-centre work.

Heavy gripper jaws with a modified chuck key.

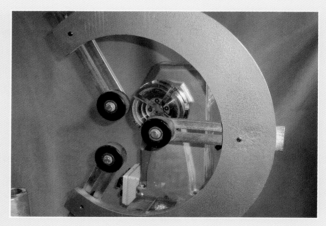

A three-point lathe steady allows tall pieces of work to be supported while they are turned.

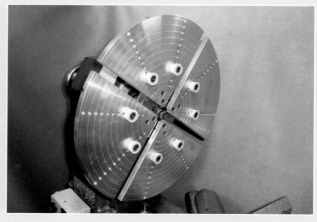

Button jaws are ideal for platter and Corian work and for off-centre turning.

JIGS

The pioneering open segmenters used a basic jig to hold individual segments in the correct position while laboriously gluing them up one-by-one.

Bill Smith (see page 14), the leading US open segmenter, still uses this technique today, employing a jig to hold the individual segments in position on his lathe and positioning them using a circular index wheel mounted behind the headstock.

In his book, *Segmented Wood Turning*, Bill Smith outlines how to build his jig, successfully gluing individual segments with modern aliphatic yellow adhesives that grab within a few seconds.

A simple open-segment jig with a circular index wheel and location guides.

TEMPLATES

The alternative is to use a template to hold a complete ring of segments together for a single glue-up. There are basically two types of template available: the fixed width, which gives a constant gap no matter what the diameter of the ring, and the angular template, which gives a variable gap dependent on the diameter of the ring. The variable-width template has a more pleasing effect on structures such as bowls; the fixed-width template is very effective on tall, thin structures such as candlesticks.

A fixed-width template for open-segment work can be made from MDF using strips of plastic as separators. A fixed-width template is developed in the Skeleton Candlesticks project (see page 155). Jerry Bennett's SegEasy angular template holds all 18 or 24 segments in a ring for gluing up a complete level at the same time. The jig accurately spaces the segments with a uniform 4° angle which results in a variable gap width depending on the diameter of the segment ring. In the absence of any other variable-width templates, I machined my own 8- and 12-segment templates out of nylon culinary cutting boards.

The variable-width SegEasy template and the fixed-width home-made template.

TOOLS

Because there is a vast array of different turning tools that cannot all be covered here, I have only included the main essentials for closed- and open-segment work in both wood and plastics. Tool technology is changing rapidly and I have therefore included modern hollowing tools and tungsten-tipped tools in this section.

Woodturners are always buying new tools.

BOWL GOUGE

The first tool that I started to use when taking up turning 12 years ago was the bowl gouge. It is still the tool that I use the most. It is, of course, ideal for segmented turning but not in its conventional bevel-rubbing method of operation; it is used in a shear-scraping mode for segmented turning. If you use it in its conventional bevel-rubbing mode the edge soon burns a small V cut. Some say that this effect is caused by the rings of glue, but that does not explain why it stays sharp in the shear-scraping mode.

The normal bowl grind works fine when shear scraping the outside of segmented objects, but a swept-back fingernail grind is needed for internal shear scraping. The insides of open-segment objects are best turned by hollowing tools and teardrop scrapers. The bowl gouge does not work on Corian because this material quickly blunts it, so tungsten-tipped tools and negative-rake scrapers are used instead.

The bowl gouge is used in shear-scraping mode for segmented turning.

Scrapers

Conventionally the scraper is used for shear scraping, not, however, held flat on the toolrest as normal, but at 45°. The cut is a slice that puts no pressure on the delicate segmented structure. If the scraper is held flat it will dig into the workpiece and usually cause a catastrophe.

There are some specialist versions designed for shear scraping that set the 45° angle automatically and these may be easier to use than the normal flat scraper. It is wise to lightly grind the edges off the back of the scraper to prevent them marking the toolrest in shear-scraping mode.

The normal 90° rake on the scraper will work when shear-scraping the outside of the segmented piece, but an 80° grind is better for shear scraping the inside of the segmented object. The 80° grind also works well on the outside. The bevel can be honed as it loses its edge rather than re-ground each time. A conventionally ground scraper works on Corian, but a negative-raked grind works better (see below).

The half-round scraper has a normal 80° grind.

Specialist shear scrapers

These are specialist tools designed to refine a surface after shaping. They enable the cutter to be presented at a shearing angle in order to sever the fibres of the wood cleanly, although they also work well on manmade materials such as acrylics and Corian.

There are various designs, some are a solid bar with a variety of tip shapes while others have removable tips, some of which can be rotated to present a

different-shaped edge to the work. The tips are usually either HSS (high-speed steel) or carbide. They are great for removing tool marks and ridges

formed during the shaping process. A diamond honing file is ideal for keeping most of them sharp, without the need to re-grind each time.

The teardrop scraper is designed to soften the curve on the inside of the segmented object.

Negative-rake scraper

The negative-rake scraper defies the logic of cutting; it is a conventional scraper with a 20–35° grind on its top edge. The scraper is held horizontally to the toolrest, the negative rake sloping down to the wood. When used flat on the toolrest this grind minimizes the risk of dig-in and puts no pressure on the object. The burr on the scraper does all the work, so it is a fine, slow-cutting action, ideal for the finishing cut on delicate objects.

The negative-rake scraper has a 20° grind on its top edge.

The inside of slender objects can be finished off with (from top to bottom) a side scraper, a flat-end scraper and a half-round scraper.

I use a flat-end scraper and have also used this technique on a half-round scraper and a side scraper for finishing the inside of slender objects such as candlesticks. The negative-rake scraper works well on acrylics and Corian too.

Negative-rake scraper

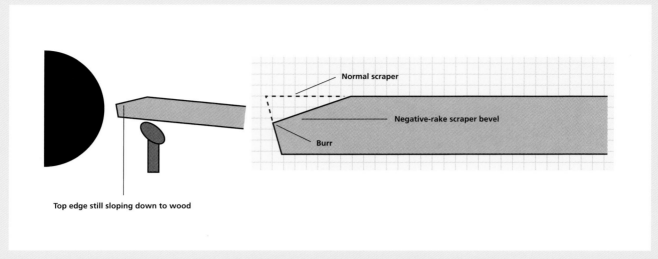

Normal scraper

Negative-rake scraper bevel

Burr

Top edge still sloping down to wood

The negative-rake scraper is held horizontally to the toolrest so the negative rake slopes down to the wood.

Tungsten carbide-tipped (TCT) ring tools

More tungsten-tipped tools are being developed for woodturning. Some feature tungsten tips brazed onto steel shanks. Others have replaceable tungsten tips that are screwed onto a range of shafts. Some are available

The tungsten-tipped ring tool shear-scraper is naturally set at 45° for shear-scraping mode.

as shear cutting tools too, but all these tools can also be used to remove wood rather than just refine it. The tungsten-tipped ring tool shear scraper is naturally set at 45° for shear-scraping mode and is ideal

for gouging out the inside of wood, acrylics and Corian objects. It keeps its edge much longer than conventional HSS tools, and its small cutting edge provides a very clean cut.

The ring tools use a small, round tungsten ring that is secured to the tool by a set screw. The tungsten ring cannot be re-sharpened without specialist tools. It is inexpensive and designed to be gradually rotated on the toolholder until blunt all round. It is then discarded.

Hollowing tool

There are various hollowing tools available on the market and they work well on removing the bulk of material from inside segmented objects. They are primarily designed for end-grain hollow forms so are well suited to the mixed grain direction of segmented objects.

Some hollowing tools have tungsten tips while others have specially shaped cutters with a limiter to determine

the thickness of the cut. The example pictured below is a specially designed hook tool with limiter. The cutter is best sharpened by a diamond honing file.

Hollowing tools are ideal for wood but usually are not very suitable for use on acrylics and Corian.

A hollowing tool removes the bulk of material from inside segmented objects.

MATERIALS

Segmenters are like artists – always trying out new materials.

The choice of materials that can be used for segmenting is vast. The main requirements are that the material can be glued and that it is stable. However, this means that green or wet timber should not be used, as it will deform and crack as it dries. Some plastics, such as synthetic polymers, including nylon, which cannot be glued, are also unsuitable.

Seasoned hardwoods are ideal for segmenting.

WOODS

Hardwoods are preferable to softwoods especially for open-segment work. It is important that the woods used for segmenting are cured and dried before use. Any movement in the timber will affect the structure of the segmented piece.

When mixtures of different types of wood are used in the same composite object, then their relative properties should be similar. This is because changes in the humidity of the surroundings will have a significant effect on the stability of the segmented object. A dense wood that hardly changes with humidity should not be mixed with a lighter, porous wood, that changes considerably with humidity, because the segments will break apart.

Segmenters undertaking complex laminate designs use a wide range of hardwoods very successfully. However, some woods are unsuitable for open segment work. They may be fibrous, such as black palmira (*Caryota urens*) with no cross-grain strength. They may be very hard and brittle, such as East Indian ebony (*Diospyrus melanoxylon*) – making retention of a clean edge on open segments very difficult. They may move with changes in humidity, such as the eucalypt, blue gum (*Eucalyptus globulus*), which is quite unstable. They may split on drying like fruit woods, olive wood (*Olea europaea*) and yew (*Taxus baccata*), and become unsuitable for open-segment work.

As a general rule, always let newly purchased wood stabilize in the workshop for a few weeks before it is used for segmenting. Humidity changes frequently in the UK so my workshop has a dehumidifier to ensure constant dryness.

LAMINATES

Some early segmented work involved gluing plywood sheets together. This technique is still used today to construct unusual or artistic shapes. It is important that the plywood used is of a good quality, as some of the cheaper versions, used for building construction, are compressed softwood with many voids.

Plywood is supplied for different uses, such as outdoor or marine. It is also supplied in different classes, determined for example by the number of knots in the surface. Good-quality hardwood plywood is recommended for building up laminate composites.

A wide variety of different woods can be used to create unique objects.

Cherry, ash, ebony and sycamore as used in the projects.

Plywood used in laminating needs to be of good quality.

ACRYLICS

Some plastics, such as acrylics, are widely used by pen makers, and these materials are also available in sheet form. They can make an interesting feature ring in wooden objects and can also be glued to the wood using CA glues. Plexiglass is ideal for laminating; offcuts can be bought from online auction sites, such as eBay.

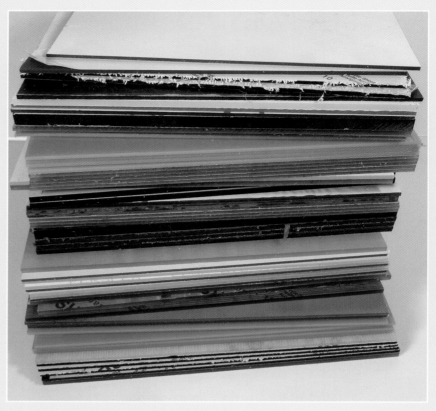

This stack of Plexiglass was bought from an online auction.

CORIAN

Corian is the brand name for a stone-like surface material created by DuPont. It is composed of acrylic polymer and alumina trihydrate. Its primary use is in kitchen worktops, bathroom vanity tops and wall cladding in showers. Corian's versatility allows it to be joined, shaped and finished into a wide variety of products. It comes in more than 100 colours and patterns.

Unless you are an approved Corian fabricator, you are not allowed to purchase Corian or its specialist glues directly from the distributors. However, most big towns have a kitchen worktop manufacturer that normally has a lot of offcuts. Alternatively, you can buy offcuts from online sites such as eBay.

Corian can be glued with CA adhesives very successfully, but the action of these instant glues leaves little time to set up and position a ring of segments. Corian can also be glued with two-part epoxy resin glues. Because these do not set quickly, the segments can be positioned easily. However, the glue line is visible when cured. In my opinion, the best glue is DuPont's own Corian epoxy, which is colour-matched to the material and cannot be seen afterwards.

Corian comes in various colours.

Adhesives

A vast array of glues is available for wood and plastics, but for segmenting you will mainly need white PVA, yellow aliphatic and instant CA adhesives.

Glue technology has changed significantly over the last 30 years. Instead of hide glue, which was heated in a water boiler, there are now ready mixed glues. Today's glues are stronger than the wood itself, as we can see with laminated wood being used for supporting beams in major construction projects. Some glues set in a few minutes and are automatically mixed with the hardener as they are squeezed out of specialist dispensers. Some can set instantly, such as the CA glues with their activators. Others, such as contact glues, require a few minutes in the air before they are brought together for instant bond.

There is no universal glue that is used for segmented turning. That is why I have selected the main glues that segmenters are likely to use and explain their unique characteristics.

PVA is a white glue that dries clear, so is ideal for open-segment work.

Polyvinyl acetate (PVA)

White PVA glues are widely used for woodwork. Unfortunately, they do not glue end grain as well as the aliphatic resin glues and are not recommended for closed-segment work, although they are fine for open-segment construction.

The brand that I use dries clear, which is ideal for not showing any glue line in open-segment work. The glue contracts on curing and is therefore unsuitable for filling voids. The glue has an initial tack after 15 minutes, but takes up to 24 hours to be fully cured.

PVA glue can be cleaned up with a wet cloth and some can be waterproof after curing. PVA is not suitable for use with acrylics or Corian.

ALIPHATIC RESIN (YELLOW)

Yellow aliphatic resin glues are ideal for gluing end grain, the preferred segment-ring construction in closed-segment work. The brand that I use also has a very quick initial tack, enabling the piece to be positioned with finger pressure for a few seconds. Unfortunately, the light yellow glue leaves a darker yellow glue line after the glue has cured, which can be seen on lighter woods. A brown version is available for darker-coloured woods but there is no lighter-colour version.

When the glue is dry it is stronger than the wood itself; the wood gives way before the glue on thin-segmented structures. These yellow glues are the strongest wood adhesives that I have used but they are not suitable for acrylics or Corian. Because the glue contracts on curing it is also unsuitable for filling voids.

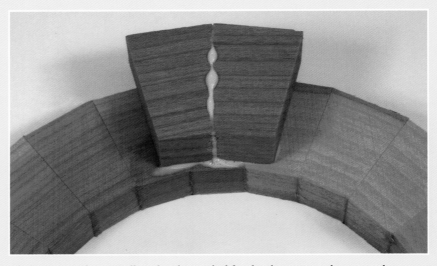

Aliphatic resin glue is a yellow glue that is ideal for closed-segment end-grain work.

The glue has an initial tack after 30 seconds but takes up to 24 hours to be fully cured.

Aliphatic resin glue can be cleaned up with a wet cloth, and some brands can be waterproof after curing. Some brands are thixotropic, meaning that they tend to run out of the joint so are unsuitable for segmenting.

Make sure that you wear disposable safety gloves when you are applying aliphatic glues.

POLYURETHANE (PU)

Polyurethane glues are used for woodwork and are unusual because of their foaming action when they come into contact with humid air. In dry climates the wood may need to be dampened before gluing to aid the curing process. The foaming action requires the joint to be clamped otherwise it is forced apart. The joint is strong but the foam can often be seen between badly fitting joints. The glue requires clamping for 30 minutes to gain a tack and needs up to eight hours to become fully cured.

These glues are very strong and waterproof. They can be used to adhere a wide range of surfaces, including wood and plastics, but are not recommended for segmented work.

PU glues are strong, but are not suitable for segmenting as they foam and need clamping.

Polyurethane glues are messy. They stain the skin and are very difficult to remove; methylated spirit or acetone are best while the glue is still uncured.

Make sure you wear disposable safety gloves, to stop the glue coming into contact with the skin.

Cyanoacrylate (CA)

CA glues form the emergency repair kit for segmented turners. While these glues are not normally used for the main construction of wooden segmented objects, they are used to fill voids and repair errant segments as the pieces are constructed.

The great advantage of these glues is their almost instant gluing ability. By using their specialist activator the segment can be set in position and instantly glued. CA glue is also good at filling any voids that may occur with badly fitting segments. The glue is very strong but brittle and does not shrink very much on curing.

CA glues come in different consistencies: thin, medium and thick. The thin glue is ideal for penetrating fine fissures and hardening spalted wood, but be careful because it creeps everywhere. The medium glue is the general-purpose adhesive for gluing errant segments and the thick variety is used for its gap-filling properties. Some fillers can be mixed with the glues to colour or toughen them for gap filling.

Dependent on its thickness, CA glue will usually dry in a few minutes without an activator, but an instant bond can be achieved by spraying the activator on one surface and spreading the glue on the other, then mating the two. Some activators can leave a white powdery film after use, which may be a problem with open-segment work.

While in the main these CA glues are instant, glue that has been trapped between levels may take a little time to cure naturally, so beware when turning newly glued areas – the glue can spit out into your face.

These adhesives are ideal for gluing acrylics and Corian as well as wood. Many segmenters use the medium CA glue for all their Corian gluing because it leaves a fine clear glue line.

Beware: these are dangerous glues. They give off a toxic vapour when curing and can bond skin instantly. A de-bonding gel is available if you get your fingers stuck together, which we all do once! But the de-bonder is not instant and takes a long time to break down the glue joint. Disposable safety gloves should always be worn to stop the glues coming into contact with the skin.

CA glues are clear and fast setting.

Two-part epoxy resin

Waterproof and strong, two-part epoxy resin glues are used extensively in the boat-building industry. The glue does not shrink on drying, but in some cases it can run out of the joint. The joint has to be fixed, but not clamped, for at least two hours and the glue requires up to eight hours to become fully cured.

These glues can also be used for acrylics and Corian, but can leave a coloured glue line unless the glue itself is coloured. The proprietary glue supplied by the manufacturer of Corian for its materials is a two-part epoxy that is colour-matched to different shades of Corian.

After curing, the glue line cannot be seen, but in gluing up wide surfaces air bubbles can be trapped, resulting in voids in the finished shape. Sometimes these can be filled afterwards with the same glue if the gap is wide enough. To avoid squeeze-out, it is important that no clamping pressure is applied when gluing up levels of work.

Beware: these are also dangerous glues to use. They give off a toxic vapour when curing and can bond and stain the skin. Disposable safety gloves should always be worn to stop the glues coming into contact with the skin.

Two-part epoxy resin is strong and waterproof.

TECHNIQUES

Solid segment

The most widely used form of segmenting is solid segmenting, where the segments are glued together – end-grain to end-grain.

The construction of composite objects by gluing material together is not new. Over the last 15 years there has been a rise in the technique of gluing segments of wood in a stacked-ring construction, which I refer to in this book as closed-segment construction. Some of these composites are made from a single variety of wood while others use different coloured woods to provide ornate patterns.

The resulting composite designs are not limited by the piece of timber being turned but only by your imagination. There have been some remarkably big composite objects produced using this technique.

'Zig Zag' by Charles Faucher.

DESIGN

Composites can be constructed on the fly, but most segmenters prepare a sectional diagram of the piece before starting. It enables the sizes of the segments to be calculated before cutting, rather than sizing them by trial and error. The design will determine the thickness of each layer and the width of each segment layer. The rough shape of the bowl is drawn showing the bowl wall thickness. An allowance for turning is added (padding) so that the segment widths can be approximated. Any feature rings or veneers can be shown on the diagram.

The easiest way to draw a design is by using squared paper.

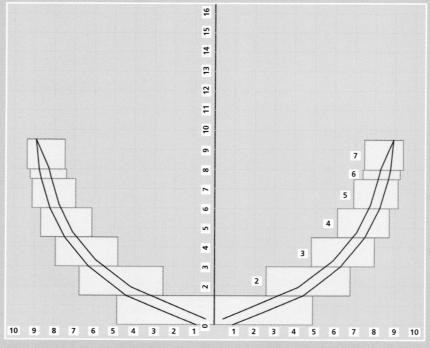

Preparation of a sectional diagram enables the sizes of the segments to be calculated.

DOING THE MATHS

Calculating the mitre angle for cutting the segments is easy enough. But the maths to calculate the length of the segments is a bit more complicated.

The segment angle is determined by dividing the number of segments into 360°. The angle for the mitre cut is then half of the segment angle.

See table below left.

Segment length
  = TAN (mitre angle) x radius of the segment ring x 2

Therefore, for the 5in ring radius with 12 segments (mitre angle 15°).

Segment length
  = TAN (15°) x 5 x 2 = 2.7in

12 segments	18 segments	24 segments
= 360°/12	= 360°/18	= 360°/24
= 30° segments	= 20° segments	= 15° segments
= 15° mitre angle	= 10° mitre angle	= 7.5° mitre angle

Solid segmenting

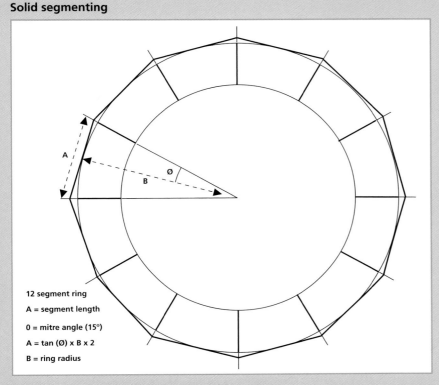

12 segment ring
A = segment length
0 = mitre angle (15°)
A = tan (Ø) x B x 2
B = ring radius

Working out segment length can be done with trigonometry.

For those of us, like me, that gave up trigonometry 50 years ago when leaving school, a simplified form of the calculation is shown below. This gives an approximate segment length without using trig functions.

Approximate segment length
  = (Diameter of the segment ring) x π / (Number of segments)

Therefore for the 10in diameter ring with 12 segments where π = 3.146

Approximate segment length
  = 10in x 3.146 / 12
  = 2.6in

For those of us not wanting to get the calculator out there are a number of free calculators on the Internet.

COMPUTER-AIDED DESIGN (CAD) SOFTWARE

Most segmenters use simple software design programs to automate the design process. This software will help in the design of the object, assist with producing flowing curves using the Bézier principle, as well as undertake all the calculations correctly. So, for the basic block diagram shown on the previous page, the design software will produce a cutting list.

There are several products on the market, some for basic open- and closed-segment design and others for the more complex ornamental designs. Be aware, however, that some products only design and do not undertake the segment calculations. They are all designed for novices; you do not have to be a computer expert to use them.

One of the features of these segmenting programs is their ability to calculate the length of the board that is required for each segment ring – a facility that is great when machining the wood beforehand. They also automatically calculate the padding – the extra wood that is built into the design to assist with the turning.

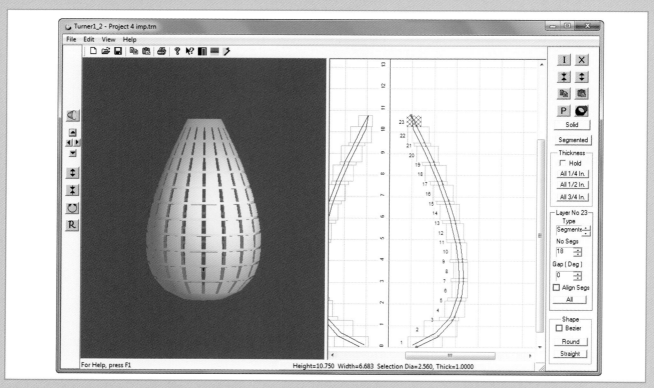

Use of a software design program makes life much easier. This example is for the Open-Segment Flower Vase on page 127.

Layer no.	No. of segments		Outer radius	Inner radius	Length	Width	Mitre angle	Gap angle	Vessel radius	Board thickness	Board length	Edge radius
Base			Solid layer 9.319 diameter x 1.500 thickness									
2	12		6.804	2.552	3.646	4.252	15.000	0.000	6.304	1.500	34.640	7.044
3	12		7.981	4.828	4.277	3.153	15.000	0.000	7.481	1.500	45.451	8.263
4	12		8.718	6.130	4.672	2.589	15.000	0.000	8.218	1.500	51.853	9.026
5	12		9.159	6.917	4.908	2.242	15.000	0.000	8.659	1.500	55.711	9.482
6	12		9.254	7.378	4.959	1.876	15.000	0.000	8.754	0.500	57.397	9.580
Top	12		9.406	7.481	5.041	1.925	15.000	0.000	8.906	1.500	58.232	9.738

The Woodturner Studio CAD program simplifies the maths. Measurements are in inches. This example is for the Segmented Bowl on page 81.

CONSTRUCTING THE BASE

It is only now, after about 15 years of turning segmented objects, that I need to review the way that their bases are built. This is because many of my early bases have cracked or the segments have parted. The early glues were not as accommodating to the movement of the wood due to drying out or humidity changes as modern adhesives are, so in some cases the wood has either cracked or the segments have come apart. In one of my early pieces the wood was very thick and possibly not as well seasoned as it should have been; it later cracked.

Thick bases tend to crack as they dry out.

SEGMENTED BASE

The photo below shows the base of my first bowl, made 12 years ago. The segments have parted. There are many reasons for this, from changes in humidity to the strength of the glue that I used. The technical reason for the failure of the segments at the centre is that wood shrinks and expands when it dries and absorbs humidity (hydroscopic). The change of the radial dimension (width) of wood is greater than the change in longitudinal dimension (length). The segment width will change more than the segment length with changes in humidity or seasoning. For a thin-walled segment it does not show up but for a wide segment, as used on the base of a vessel, the change in shape will reveal itself.

The answer is simple: do not make the base layer out of segments but from a solid piece of seasoned wood. Of course, some turners will say that may spoil the look of the finished object, and that is why some segmenters use the floating-base technique, as explained on the following page.

Made 12 years ago, the segments on my bowl have parted.

SOLID BASE

Since my early disasters I have been using solid bases, but even these will not always eliminate cracks and broken joints. The consensus in the segmenting community is that the solid base should not be more than 5in (125mm) in diameter. Ideally the wood should be quarter-sawn (see diagram) to ensure an even edge-on grain pattern with no knots or shakes. The most important requirement, however, is that the wood be completely seasoned and dry before being used.

By using a solid base, the inside can be turned to match the vessel's interior shape. The underside can be hollowed in the middle to ensure the vessel does not wobble. Both of these factors will go some way to minimizing any cracking or warping of the base.

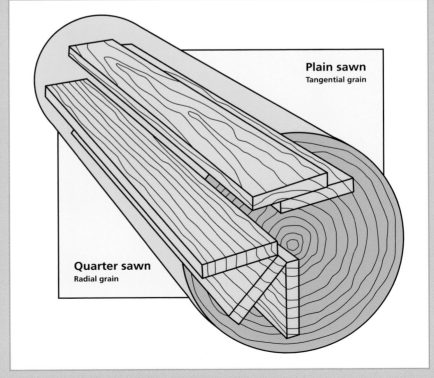

Timber must be completely dry before it is used.

Floating segment base

For many years Malcolm Tibbetts has been advocating the advantages of the floating-ring technique. It allows for the outside of the segmented piece to have segments showing at the base, but these segments are in a ring supporting a floating disc on the inside of the base – using the same concept as the floating panel in old-fashioned solid-wood doors. There is enough movement in the rebate to allow the outside segmented ring and the inner disc to move independently.

His recommended approach to the floating-ring technique is shown in the diagrams. A tapered rebate is cut in the base ring to accept the disc – with a sufficient gap between both to allow for movement – then a second smaller tapered ring is constructed to act as a keeper ring, allowing the disc to move freely. The keeper ring is carefully glued in place – but ensuring that no glue gets onto the floating disc. The disc should move easily after gluing.

Floating base construction

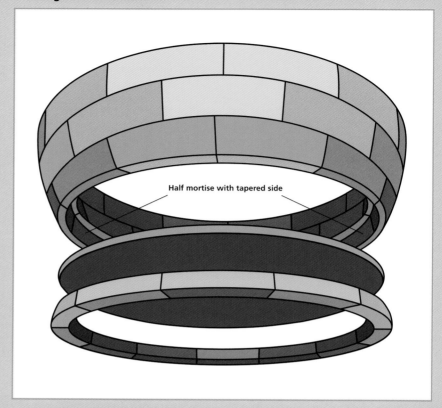

Malcolm Tibbett's approach to the floating-ring technique.

Floating base cross-view

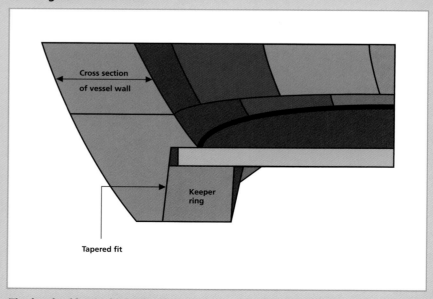

The disc should move freely after gluing.

WOODEN FACEPLATE WITH PAPER JOINT

If the solid base is made from the same thickness of material as the segments, then there is no scope for the base to be parted off. By using a wooden faceplate to fit the chuck, the solid base can be glued to the faceplate with a paper joint to enable easy separation later. There is no need to part off valuable solid-base material. My wooden faceplates have been made from scrap timber. They are turned to be ⅜in (10mm) larger than my chuck diameter, with a dovetail cut on the back to be held in the chuck. They are then fitted to the chuck and faced ready to accept the paper joint.

I mark the top of the faceplate with the top of the chuck; this technique allows me to interchange many pieces in progress, always into the same position. After the workpiece is finished the joint is broken with a knife and the faceplate re-faced ready to be used again.

Ensure the wooden faceplate surface is flat before gluing up.

TIP: Since we will be reverse chucking many of the projects it is a good idea to have a centre hole in the back of the wooden faceplate to centre on the tailstock. I drill out my faceplates with a ¹⁹⁄₃₂in (15mm) Forstner bit to accept support from the shoulder of my revolving tailstock.

Use of a wooden faceplate to the fit the chuck allows the solid base to be glued to the faceplate with a paper joint that can be easily separated later.

The wooden faceplate.

Cutting wood into strips

Using the circular saw to cut strips.

Many segmenters use kiln-dried ready-planed wood for segmenting. I rarely buy new wood; the wood that I mainly use comes from trees that have been felled in my garden and then planked by a local wood yard, so it is rough sawn and rarely flat. Before I can start to dimension my timber I have to achieve a straight edge and then face and edge it on the jointer. I will assume for this book that flat-sawn timber is being used.

Planing

My first planer thicknesser had two planing blades. When I upgraded to my jointer and thicknesser machines they had three blades. If the blades are set correctly the three-blade system gives a smoother finish than the two-blade set-up. Setting the blades is a time-consuming chore, but when undertaken correctly gives impressive results. Different planers have different techniques for setting the blades – one day I would like a planer that has automatic setting blades!

Before operating, the back fence needs to be checked to ensure it is at 90° to the bed. The blade protector should be used over flat timber and butted up to the side when edging.

Several light cuts are preferable to fewer deeper cuts because the latter tear the grain around knots and heavily figured hardwoods.

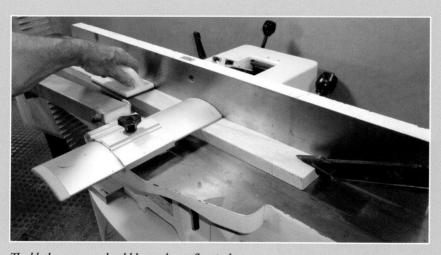

The blade protector should be used over flat timber…

… and butted up to the side when edging.

TIP: Always mark the face and edge after planing – it is surprising how easy it is to get the wrong edge later.

SAWING

To get the best out of a circular saw, the wood must be faced and edged beforehand. The face side is placed down on the circular saw table and the planed edge towards the saw fence. Circular saws are never accurate – mine seems to cut in a slight arc, so I set the saw fence to give a small amount of extra width for finishing off on the planer. If a second strip of wood is to be cut from the salvage left over from the last cut, plane the edge square again first. It is worth checking periodically that the saw blade is at 90° to the table, as it can easily be thrown out of adjustment.

TIP: Modern circular saws need to have full extraction for the sawdust otherwise they can clog and burn the wood. The extraction is needed to remove sawdust not only from under the saw table but also from above the blade.

SAFETY ADVICE: Recent statistics show that the most dangerous piece of equipment for the home user is the circular saw, so every precaution should be taken to ensure push-sticks are used instead of fingers near the blade.

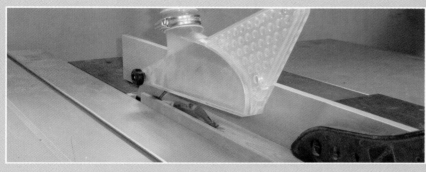

Use a push-stick to feed the wood into the saw.

Push the cut length past the cutting blade to avoid kick-back.

Cut all the lengths you require at the same time.

THICKNESSING

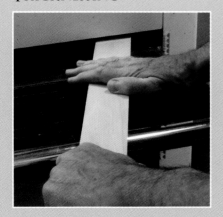

Take several lighter cuts on the thicknesser rather than deeper ones.

Because the accuracy and evenness of the timber strip thickness is very important in segmenting, cut all the strips and thickness them together using the same setting.

One of the problems with machine thicknessing is snipe – a wave formed in the timber as the blade jumps and digs in at the start or finish of thicknessing. Expensive thicknessers have additional feed rollers to eliminate this problem. To minimize the chance of snipe, start the timber off at an angle rather than end-on; to stop it jerking up, press it flat to the in-table as it is fed in.

As with the planer, the setting of the blades is critical. My three-blade thicknesser is easier to set up than the planer. I have never had to change the parallel setting of the rollers, but I know that they can be adjusted. Again, several lighter cuts work much better on some timbers than deeper cuts.

CUTTING SEGMENTS

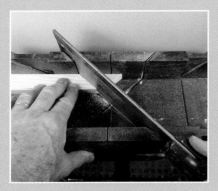

Cutting mitres using a mitre block and tenon saw.

The essential part of segmenting is the ability to cut segments accurately. Cutting discrepancies cannot be covered over with thick glue or eliminated by compressing the timber joint to make it fit.

HANDSAWING

Most joiner's mitre guides have both 90° and 45° pre-set angles. The first project, for a simple closed-segment bowl, uses a 15° mitre angle, so a basic joiner's mitre guide is not suitable. This problem, however, can easily be solved by use of a picture-framing mitre guide – much cheaper than an electric mitre saw – but be prepared for some painstaking work.

BANDSAWING

This is the technique that I used until I bought a modern mitre saw. The bandsaw is a very safe means of cutting segments and I still use it for cutting thin ones.

To use the equipment, fix a salvage fence made from scrap hardwood to the mitre fence to enable the angled cut to penetrate the wooden fence. This allows the cut segment to be pushed past the cutting edge of the blade to clear it for the next segment to be cut. To support the segment and avoid jamming the blade, the mitre fence is set at an obtuse angle to the fence.

An engineer's square is used to check the blade for vertical, then the wood is fed into the saw and the segments cut. The wood is turned over after each cut to achieve the maximum number of segments from the smallest piece of timber. Grain direction will change slightly using this principle, so for heavily featured strips consider cutting all the segments the same way.

The mitre fence does not have to be accurate because the segments will be accurately cleaned up on the disc sander afterwards. It is important to check the 90° angle of the blade and the mitre angle. The simplest way is to cut some segments from scrap wood to make a semi-circle – they never come together as a straight edge the first time.

For support, set the mitre fence at an obtuse angle to the fence.

If grain direction is important, cut all the segments the same way.

If the bandsaw burr on the trailing edge is not removed before sanding, it will affect the accuracy of the finished sanded angle. Some segmenters use sandpaper, but I prefer to use a small warding file to remove the burr.

Check the blade for vertical using an engineer's square.

As an alternative to sandpaper, remove the burr with a small warding file.

Disc sanding

Before you use the disc sander it is important to check the face is square. Start by setting it vertical using an engineer's square, then finally adjust the angle by hand using a scrap piece of wood.

The coarseness of the sanding disc – the most suitable for fine segmenting is 120 grit – will pull the segment in. The correct angle is normally less than 90°, depending on the type of wood and its thickness.

The mitre fence setting has to be very accurate, so I invested in a replacement specialist mitre fence with many pre-set angles, to replace the basic mitre fence supplied with the sander. A false mitre fence backplate is prepared from salvage hardwood to the correct angle for the mitre, with a fine clearance to the sanding disc. This will support the segments correctly when sanding.

A sliding depth stop will also be required to ensure the segment remains square and is not sanded too small. I usually make the mitre fence and sliding depth stop as a pair and store them away afterwards for possible later reuse.

Segmenters have many different ways of sanding their segments. Over the years I have found that a depth stop is needed to prevent the segments from being cut back too far. I have also found that it is better to support the long edge of the segment on the mitre fence rather than the shorter edge; this ensures that both edges are cut accurately with reference to the long (outside) edge. It is surprising how segments can be pulled away from the mitre fence by the force of the sanding disc.

To check the accuracy of the mitre angle, cut some scrap pieces of wood to create either a right angle or a semi-circle. Once all the segment angles have been checked, the segments can be sanded.

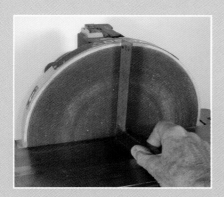

First set the face vertical using an engineer's square.

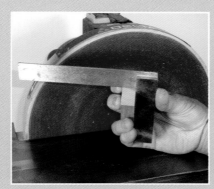

Adjust the angle by hand using a scrap piece of wood.

A mitre fence and sliding depth stop made as a pair could be used again.

Make a right angle or a semi-circle from scrap timber and use it to check mitre angle accuracy.

The segments are sanded after the angles are checked.

SAFETY ADVICE: Sanding dust can be a health hazard and these sanding machines need good vacuum extraction. The disc will sometimes get clogged with resinous dust, which can easily be removed with a rubber disc cleaner.

Mitre sawing

Modern mitre saws can give an exceptionally clean cut without the need for any further de-burring or sanding, but they usually have a metal backplate with a cut-out for the blade that is wide enough for the blade to clear all compound angles. That gap in the backplate provides little support for small segments so these can fly off – often getting sucked into the dust extractor.

You will need a properly set blade and a tight-fitting backplate. A piece of scrap hardwood is cut and bolted onto the backplate, covering the blade cut-out. The mitre saw is set to the correct angle and then allowed to cut a clean slot in the wooden backplate. This continuous backplate gives excellent support for even small segments as well as ensuring a clean exit cut requiring no de-burring afterwards. Since different segment angles will be required, a new false backplate made from scrap should be fitted for each angle rather than reusing an old backplate cut for a different mitre angle.

When my new mitre saw was delivered there was movement in the bearings supporting the swinging arm. This was eliminated by adjustment, giving a very accurate cut through its axis. Check for vertical alignment using an engineer's set square, and double check on a cut segment.

Before starting ensure that the blade is accurately set vertical and all adjusters tightened. This gives a very clean and accurate slot for the blade to pass through, minimizing any burr on the back edge of the segment. A vertical blade also helps to ensure that the segment will not normally fly off.

An end stop is required for accurate segment width measurement. The mitre angle on the end stop is cut using the mitre saw and then repositioned on the far side of the blade. The segment width can be accurately measured using a small steel rule; a sample segment is cut to ensure correct dimensions and a square face.

Some segmenters use a manual hold-down device to stop the segments flying off. This means that the rest of the wood is unsupported. I prefer to hold the longer length of wood in one hand and the mitre saw handle in the other. It is wrong to cut small pieces of wood in such a way that the fingers are in close proximity to the blade. Your fingers are more valuable than the segments!

A clean cut can be obtained by slowly lowering the mitre saw on the wood. Because the 90° set of the blade can easily be knocked out of adjustment if a segment is caught, ensure that the blade stops before it is retracted after the cut.

Test the accuracy of the mitre angle by cutting off enough segments to make a right angle or a semi-circle. The back fence may require slight adjustment so that the mitre scale reads accurately. Make sure you check the segment dimensions and faces before starting to cut.

Check for vertical using an engineer's set square...

... and double check on a cut segment.

Cut a sample segment to check that the dimensions are correct and the face is square.

Lower the mitre saw onto the wood.

Make sure the blade stops before it is retracted from the cut segment.

Check segment dimensions and faces before commencing cutting.

CREATING SEGMENT RINGS

As discussed in the previous chapter, the most suitable glue for closed-segment work is the yellow, aliphatic resin type, which has the strength for gluing together end-grain woods.

Some turners use presses or steel bands to compress the segments when gluing. Unfortunately, the wood tries to reconstitute its original shape afterwards and the joints can separate. A much more reliable method is to use no pressure at all. Using the tack properties of the yellow glues, each segment can be manually held in place while the glue tacks; just a couple of seconds is all that is required.

Glued rings are left to cure.

GRAIN DIRECTION

Before gluing the segments, ensure that the grain of the wood is in the same direction for all the segments, or alternatively conform to a pre-designed pattern – nothing looks worse than segmented vessels with the grain of the wood in random directions. Some segmenters, like Curt Theobald, pay particular attention to the grain direction of the wood when designing their pieces.

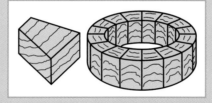

A convex grain direction will give a concave curve.

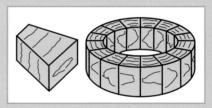

A quarter-sawn vertical grain direction will give concentric circles.

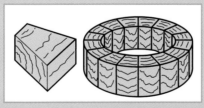

A concave grain direction will give a convex curve.

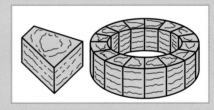

A quarter-sawn horizontal grain direction will give horizontal lines.

TIP: Sort the segments beforehand to give similar grain directions because, once the glue has been applied to the edges, checking the grain direction is difficult; a small pencil mark on the top edge of the segment helps register the top.

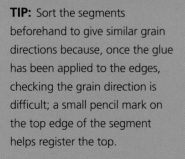

Sort the segments to give similar grain direction.

Gluing up segment rings

For reliability, spread glue on both edges before rubbing the segments together and then setting them into the correct position. This ensures that the glue is applied to both surfaces and any excess glue is squeezed out.

A flat glue brush or a fine artist's brush is ideal for spreading the glue onto the segments. A polythene sheet stretched over a flat surface like a plate of glass provides an excellent place on which to glue the rings flat without the adhesive adhering to the surface. The glued segments are allowed to cure for 20 minutes then carefully lifted off the polythene sheet to let the glue dry on the underside.

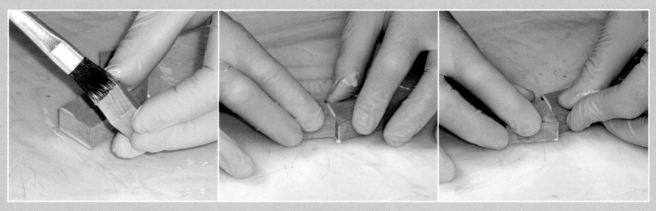

Spread the glue on both surfaces and gently rub them together until the glue grabs.

Semi-circular construction

Gluing the segments into semi-circles allows for slight discrepancies to be sanded out before completing the segment ring.

Once the semi-circles have been glued up they can be removed from the polythene backing to dry out.

When the two halves have dried – usually after about eight hours – they can be cleaned up using a sheet of sandpaper or a disc sander.

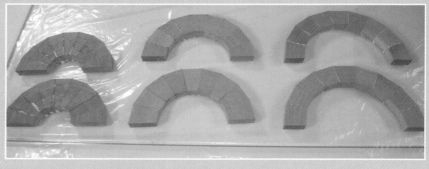

Glue the segments on a flat sheet of polythene.

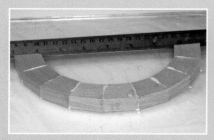

Check the first ring to ensure it is a true semi-circle.

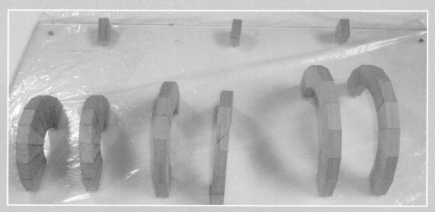

After five minutes, stand the semi-circles up to allow the glue to dry.

TRUING AND GLUING

Remove the excess glue on both surfaces and then sand the unglued edge flat. To compensate for any error in the disc sander, sand the semi-circles with opposite sides down. Match the two semi-circles to ensure that they fit together without any gap. Glue both edges and hold in position until tacked. The ring will need another eight hours for the glue to become completely dry.

Remove the excess glue on both surfaces.

Sand the edges with opposite sides down.

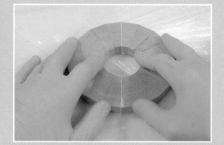
Hold the glued rings until the glue grabs.

PREPARING RINGS FOR GLUING

One surface of the glued-up rings can be sanded on a flat surface, while the other is sanded on the lathe.

Even though a considerable effort is made to ensure that the wooden segments are of a consistent thickness, when they are glued up there will be some unevenness. To ensure that the joints are clean and tight it is important that the levels are flat before they are glued together.

MANUAL SANDING

The simplest method is to sand the glued-up rings on a sheet of sandpaper on a flat surface. This can be a somewhat laborious job but only one surface needs to be sanded flat; the other can be dealt with on the lathe after gluing up.

DRUM SANDING

An easier method for flattening the segment rings is to use a drum sander. Clean off the excess glue with a light pass on both surfaces first and then take one surface down to a clean, sanded finish; the other surface can be cleaned up on the lathe after gluing up.

TIP: These sanders can remove a large amount of wood so to prevent the ring becoming too thin, take only light passes.

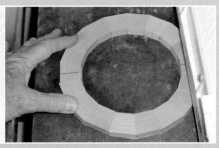

A drum sander has a healthy appetite for flattening segment rings.

CONSTRUCTING THE COMPOSITE

PREPARING THE BASE

As mentioned earlier in this section, the base level should be either solid or have a floating central segment, so before the first segment ring is glued to the base it is important to ensure that it is perfectly flat and square.

The base is spun on the lathe and a light pass is made with the bowl gouge in shear-scraping mode. The edge should be at 45° to the toolrest otherwise it will catch on the side grain. Light sweeps are made to ensure the surface is running square to the lathe and flat. A steel rule is held against the base to ensure that it is flat.

Make light sweeps to ensure the surface is flat.

Place a steel rule against the base to test for flatness.

TIP: Use a wooden faceplate in the chuck to save valuable timber.

GLUING THE FIRST RING

Spread the glue thinly and evenly over the segment ring.

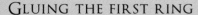

Concentric circles drawn on the backplate ensure the rings are mounted correctly.

TIP: Use only enough glue to wet the wood; excess glue will slow down the curing process and cause a mess if it drips onto the lathe bed.

Yellow glue is applied to the surface of the sanded first ring using a glue brush to ensure that the adhesive is evenly spread. Glue is then applied to the outer ring of the base. I like to support the rings using a piece of MDF glued onto a backplate – a flat disc – that can be mounted on the tailstock revolving centre. Concentric circles drawn on the backplate beforehand ensure that the segment rings are mounted concentrically.

Bring the ring and the base together and clamp them using the backplate. Ensure there is enough pressure on the tailstock to squeeze out glue all the way around the ring. The tailstock can be loosened off after about 10 minutes when the glue has tacked, to allow the wood to dry out without undue pressure. The composite can be removed from the lathe after about 30 minutes' drying time. Leave the base for at least four hours for the glue to cure completely.

Clamp the ring and base together using a backplate.

Now centralize the segment ring using the backplate.

SANDING AND GLUING EACH LEVEL

Sand each level flat before gluing the next level.

True up the outside before gluing.

Continue to build up the levels, ensuring the joints overlap brickwork fashion.

The finished composites should look like these.

The process is now repeated for each level. The glued ring is trued up on the lathe, first by a light sweeping shear scrape with the bowl gouge to ensure the surface is running true, and then with the sanding sheet, held between the backplate to ensure it is flat. Check each time by adding a concentric pencil line on the face and sanding it off.

A slight bevel is cut on the outer edge of the each level of the composite to provide a reliable true circular edge for matching to the next level, the segment rings always being slightly oval.

Glue is applied to the next segment ring and the composite top level as before. The segment ring is then positioned onto the composite using the backplate. It is important that not only is the ring concentric to the composite, but also that the individual segment glue lines match up – brickwork fashion – with equal distances between the lines.

Each level will need at least four hours' drying time. It's wise to leave the finished composite for 24 hours before turning.

TURNING THE COMPOSITE

The composite is supported at both ends.

Turning segmented composites requires a more refined turning technique than plain bowl turning. The glue used is very hard and can quickly burn the edge of the bowl gouge.

The conventional sequence of turning a normal bowl is to create the shape on the outside and then turn the inside to match that shape. With segmented composites the walls are not as strong as solid-wood structures and will need supporting to achieve a respectably thin wall thickness. This can be obtained using conventional techniques, but the composite will start to vibrate badly as the wall becomes thinner.

By hollowing the inside of the composite first, leaving the outside segments still untouched, the wall will have enough strength for the required shape to be achieved. It can then be reversed on the chuck by using a jam chuck for the top, with the face supported on the tailstock. This means that the composite is supported at both ends while it is turned to the finished thickness on the outside.

USING HOLLOWING TOOLS FOR TURNING THE INSIDE

The hollowing tool that was designed for cutting end grain in hollow forms works very well at roughing out the inside of the segmented composite structure. There are several proprietary products on the market and all work well. The one shown in the photo has an adjustable limiter that ensures the tool does not dig in and remove too much wood or fracture the composite structure.

These tools will need frequent honing as the glue will take its toll on the edge. Some are tungsten-tipped so more easily able to cope with the harder glue.

It is important that these tools are used only for roughing out the shape to size. Enough thickness must be kept to allow the finishing cuts to remove all the tool marks and ensure a smooth curve. The surface is torn and will need finishing with a tear scraper to remove the imperfections.

The hollowing tool makes light work of the inside.

The surface is very rough and needs further smoothing.

Using tungsten-tipped tools

Tungsten-tipped tools are slowly becoming more widely used for woodturning. These tools usually have a circular tip made of a tungsten-type composite that can be gradually rotated as it becomes dull and then replaced. The tips cannot be sharpened without specialist equipment, and are designed to be discarded and cheaply replaced. The tips do, however, last a long time. Tungsten-tipped shear scrapers give a very clean and accurate cut. The larger-tipped models are good for roughing out and the smaller-tipped versions for finishing. They do not burn like the bowl gouge on segment work and are ideal for work on laminates, plastics and Corian.

Tungsten-tipped tools work well on laminates, plastics and Corian.

Teardrop shear scraping

The teardrop scraper is the perfect finishing tool for the inside of the composite vessel. Its teardrop shape can be adjusted to the shape of the vessel's interior, producing a very smooth and clean cut. This tool is ideal for removing the flat spots and ridges inside the vessel that are often left after roughing out.

The teardrop scraper is used in a 45° shear-scraping mode with light cuts taken to ensure a clean finish. It is usually ground at 90°, enabling the scraper to be turned over in the tool and the second edge used before re-grinding or honing.

Use your teardrop scraper to remove internal flat spots and ridges.

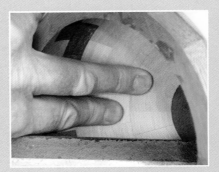

Seek out imperfections with your fingers.

TIP: Fingers are ideal for locating tool imperfections and flat spots. It is best to mark immediately with a pencil line the areas needing more attention because once the composite is spinning seeing problem areas is difficult.

TURNING THE OUTSIDE OF THE COMPOSITE

The outside of the composite bowl is a very unwelcoming surface until the edges
have been removed, but they can be cleaned up without affecting its strength.
Therefore a slow speed, of 500rpm, is selected and the rough edges removed
by either a roughing gouge or a bowl gouge.

SHEAR SCRAPING WITH THE BOWL GOUGE

Once the surface has been cleaned up
and the tool is cutting continuously
then the bowl gouge can be used in
its preferred shear-scraping mode to
tidy up the surface.

I like just to clean up the rough
edges at the top at this stage as the
thickness of the outer edge needs to
be maintained until the inside of the
composite has been shaped.

Using the bowl gouge to shear scrape the surface.

Horizontal coarse shear scraping cut with deep fluted bowl gouge

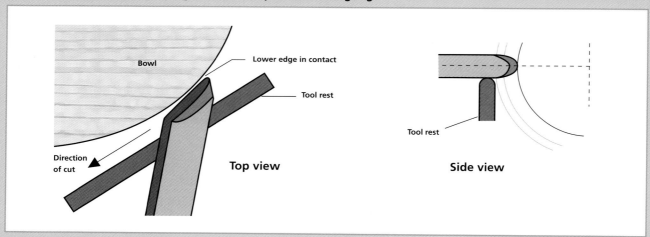

Vertical fine shear scraping cut with deep fluted bowl gouge

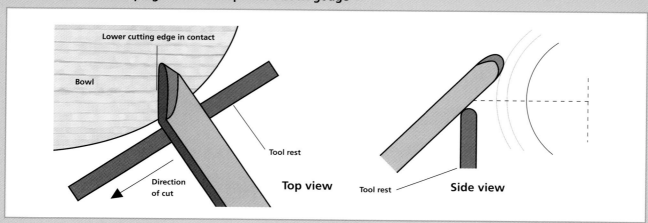

SHEAR SCRAPING

Conventional flat scrapers and specialist shear scrapers can be used for shear scraping. It is a technique that puts very little load on the work and is therefore ideal for fragile structures. Shear scrapers are normally scrapers with the cutting edge held at a 45° angle to the toolrest and workpiece.

Shear scraper cuts with a conventional scraper can leave ridges, but if the bowl gouge is used as a shear scraper it provides a clean, smooth finishing cut on the outside of the composite vessel. The bowl gouge is not recommended for shear scraping the inside of the vessel.

The technique of using the bowl gouge for shear scraping goes against all the training one had when learning how to use the bowl gouge for the first time, but once the technique is mastered, it becomes a very safe one that can be used in a wide range of applications to produce a really smooth finish.

Unfortunately, it is more a finishing technique than a roughing-out method; therefore other tools are better for roughing out the unfriendly surface of the segmented composite.

Use your shear scraper with the cutting edge held at 45° to the toolrest and workpiece.

Taking a shear-scraping cut (top view).

A bowl gouge used for shear scraping produces a smooth exterior finish.

REVERSING THE COMPOSITE

At this stage the composite is reversed on the lathe, the inside being mounted on a jam chuck and the faceplate being held in the tailstock. A simple jam chuck can be made from circles of MDF glued together and mounted on a faceplate to be held in chuck jaws constructed from scrap timber. The edges of the MDF are turned into a cone.

At this stage the false baseplate is not removed, so allowing the composite to be reversed and re-turned or sanded as required. The faceplate is mounted on the tailstock, which is tightened up to enable the composite to be turned without slippage.

Using the bowl gouge in long sweeping strokes from the rim to the middle and then from the base to the middle, the outside can now be turned to create a superb finished size and shape.

The thickness is checked consistently with callipers or by hand, using fingertip pressure.

At this stage the composite shape may have to be carefully adjusted on the inside. When the rim and sides are turned down to the correct shape the faceplate can be removed and the bottom of the vessel finished.

Since the faceplate has been glued to the bottom level with a paper joint, it is a very simple process to crack open the joint using a sharp knife blade. Position the blade edge on the paper joint and give the back of the blade a sharp tap with a hammer; the joint will break apart leaving a flat surface that can be cleaned up.

Again, the photo sequence shown here illustrates the process.

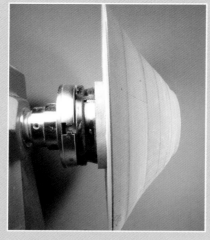

The edges of the MDF are turned into a cone.

The tailstock is tightened to allow the composite to be turned without slippage.

Using the bowl gouge in long sweeping strokes delivers superb shape and finish.

Crack open the paper joint with a sharp knife blade…

… strike the back of the blade with a hammer …

… and the joint will break apart.

COMPLETING THE BASE

The composite is remounted on the jam chuck and the faceplate centred on the tailstock with a small Sorby stebcentre, a device that hardly marks the wood.

Tailstock pressure is applied as before to prevent the composite spinning, and the base finished off. It is best to undercut the base to enable the composite to sit correctly. Only the base to the stebcentre can be cut away. A small pip – to be removed by hand later – will remain where the stebcentre is holding the base.

At this stage the outside is sanded, starting at 100 to 150 grit and working through the grits to 400. A rotating sanding disc is preferred, or the outside can be sanded by hand.

Check the outside of the composite for any tool or coarse sanding marks and, if necessary, start the process again.

Once the composite has been removed from the lathe, the pip in the base can be taken off using a wood chisel. The base is then sanded to remove any trace of the pip, starting at 150 grit and working up to 400 grit.

The small pip will be removed manually at a later point.

The outside can be sanded by disc or by hand.

Remove the pip with a carving chisel and sand.

FINISHING

Now is the time to apply the finish. Usually a sanding sealer is applied no matter what the final finish will be. Care should be taken that it is applied evenly and any excess wiped off. Leave for up to four hours to dry before applying an optional second coat of the final finish. Since most of the projects will have a lacquered finish, use a sanding sealer supplied in a spray can rather than the type that is brushed on.

Modern lacquer sprays give a very durable finish. The satin finish is sometimes preferred to the full gloss. Two to three coats will be required, leaving the lacquer to harden for at least four hours between coats. The composite will need to be de-nibbed between coats with either 400-grit sandpaper or a fine abrasive pad or wire wool. To ensure all dust is removed the composite should be wiped over with a tack cloth before the next coat of finish is applied.

The piece should finish up something like this.

OPEN SEGMENT

Open-segment construction extends the principles of closed-segment work with the introduction of gaps between the segments. The segments are therefore not glued together into a ring as in closed-segment construction, but are held in place either individually using a jig or as a complete ring using a template. The segments are glued side grain to side grain; there is no end-grain gluing, so different glues can be used, as explained later.

Open segment construction demands the use of glues other than yellow aliphatic.

DESIGN

As with closed-segment construction the design can be undertaken by hand drawing the shape and manually calculating the segment widths, but very few segmenters do this today. The type of jig used for locating the segments will determine the calculation. Some jigs have a fixed-width separator between the segments; this does not affect the segment angle. Others have an angular – variable width – separator between the segments, which does affect the segment angle. The leading CAD packages for segmented turners enable either fixed-width or angular-width segment construction.

As with a solid-segment design, start with a solid base or one with a floating centre. Finishing off the design with either a solid top or a solid segmented ring ensures strong and stable construction.

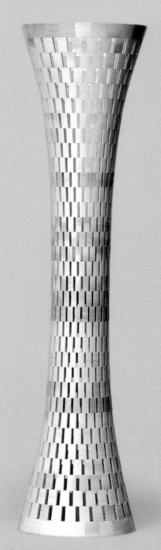

This technique can support a wall thickness as minimal as ⅛in (3mm) or less.

A variable-width and a fixed-width template.

The open-segment technique still produces exceptionally strong composite structures as long as the glue and wood are strong enough and care has been taken with construction accuracy. The great benefit of this type of construction is being able to see the thickness of the structure through the gap between the segments, at all stages of turning and finishing.

The wall thickness can be as adventurous as you feel able – having constructed these types of composite for the past 10 years, my structures have been strong even when the wall thickness has been ⅛in (3mm) or less.

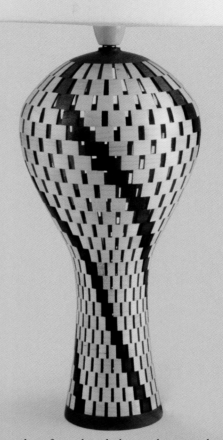

The ebony changed size faster than the boxwood, causing the spiral to split.

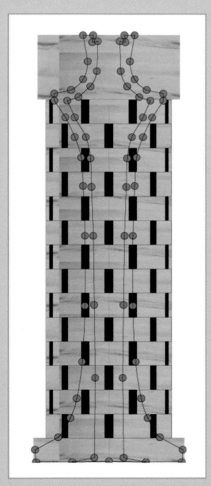

With tall composites you need a good outer radius for support during construction and internal turning.

Mixing different species of wood can lead to problems when one type has different characteristics to the other. Some timbers vary in size more than others in different humidities. The early version of the Gherkin Spiral Lamp Stand, shown above, made from ebony and boxwood, split along the spiral because the ebony changed size faster than the boxwood in differing humidities.

When constructing tall composites it is best to have a significant outer radius to support the object during the construction stage and the later turning of the inside. This will be removed when turning the outside of the composite construction, but it will give it support in the more difficult stages, as will be seen in the Open-segmented Candlesticks project on page 137, where a large outer radius is utilized in the construction. This design was developed in 3D Design Pro and Woodturner Pro.

Jigs for holding segments in place

Some segmenters still prefer to glue each open segment separately using a positioning jig, along with a graduated index wheel to locate its radial position.

Bill Smith has been the leading exponent of the single-segment positioning jig, as explained earlier. This method relies on the initial tack of the glue to hold the segment in place after positioning it. As soon as the aliphatic glue bites, the composite can be rotated for positioning the next segment.

The only variable with this method is the graduated index wheel which can easily be drawn or downloaded from Bill Smith's website and printed out. Go to www.smithart.us/download.htm. Wheel plans are available for from six to 144 segments. This technique results in the same angular-gap design as the variable-width templates discussed below.

I built my own version of a jig for gluing open segments that was bench mounted. It uses a potter's turntable as the base and a piece of slotted aluminium strip for the vertical support. The graduated index wheel was fixed to the turntable together with the wooden faceplate to hold the composite for turning later. Two arms slide up the slotted aluminium upright to indicate the position on the index wheel and the position of the segment to be glued. This arrangement works well for unusual designs that are not ideally suited to fixed templates.

Simple bench-mounted jig.

Each segment is placed individually.

Templates

The concept of the template is to position the whole ring of segments for gluing up at the same time. The template is held centrally in the tailstock, which is then drawn up to the composite, positioned and pressure applied.

There are two main types of template: fixed width, where the segment gap remains the same no matter what the radius of the ring is, and angular width, where the segment gap varies as the radius of the ring increases. Both give very different effects to the finished article.

The fixed gap template is used in the Open-segment Candlesticks Project (page 137) and the variable width template is used in the Open-segment Fruit Bowl project (page 101).

FIXED-WIDTH TEMPLATES

Fixed-width templates are fairly easy to design and build. They work well on designs with a constant diameter, like candlesticks, but not on those with an increasing diameter, like a bowl.

A fixed-width template is made in the Open-segment Candlesticks project using a ⅛in (3mm) strip of plastic as a separator, which is held in place by MDF segments.

The mitre angle is the same as for a closed segment ring:

12 segments

 = 360° / 12

 = 30° segments

 = 15° mitre angle

The segment length calculation is similar to the closed-segment design but the thickness of the separator has to be deducted from the length of the segment.

Segment length

 = (Diameter of the segment ring)

 x π / (Number of segments)

 – separator thickness.

Therefore, for the 10in (25cm) diameter ring with 12 segments and a separator thickness of ⅛in (3mm):

Approximate segment length

 = (10in x 3.146 / 12) – ⅛in

 = 2½in (6cm)

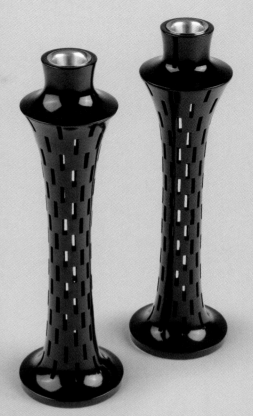

The Open-segment Candlesticks on page 137 use a fixed-width template.

Two fixed-width templates with different thickness of separators.

ANGULAR-WIDTH SEGMENT TEMPLATES

The SegEasy plate used for the Open-segment Fruit Bowl project has an angular construction. The segment separators are 4° on both the 18- and 24-segment SegEasy jigs.

An angular jig design is very difficult to build oneself and my attempts were never as accurate as the SegEasy template. The 8-segment jig that I produced is used in the Skeleton Candlesticks project on page 155.

The segment separators are 4° on both the 18- and 24-segment SegEasy jigs.

I made my own 8 and 12 angular segment templates.

The mitre angle uses the same calculation as the closed-segment design less the separator angle. For a 12 segment template with a 10° separator angle the calculation would be:

12 segments = (360° / 12 segments) – 10° (separator angle)
= 20° segments
= 10° mitre angle

An approximation of the segment length is a similar calculation to the fixed-width design but the thickness of the separator has to be allowed for. This is done as a proportion of the segment angle (the gap ratio).

Therefore, for the 10in-diameter ring with 12 segments and a separator angle of 10°, a 12-solid-segment design would have a 30° segment angle (A); the new open segment design has a 20° segment angle (B).

Open segmenting

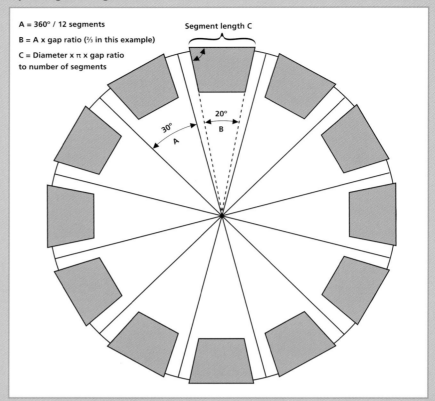

A = 360° / 12 segments
B = A x gap ratio (⅔ in this example)
C = Diameter x π x gap ratio to number of segments

Segment length C

How to calculate angular-width segments.

Gap ratio
= Open-segment angle (B) / Solid-segment angle (A)
= 20 / 30
= 0.667

Approximate segment length C
= Diameter x π x gap ratio / Number of segments
= 10in (25cm) x 3.146 x 0.667 / 12
= 1¾in (4.5cm)

COMPOSITE CONSTRUCTION TECHNIQUES

BASE

The base is very similar to those used for solid-segment construction. A solid base is preferred as long as the wood is stable and will not warp. A floating base can be used but is usually not as visually pleasing as a solid one.

Rather than waste material thickness when parting off the base, use the paper joint technique described earlier. Aliphatic, or even PVA glue, provides a strong bond between the surfaces, which must be flat beforehand. As described before, a sharp tap on a knife blade is all that is needed to separate the joint afterwards.

When making a paper joint opt for glossy paper.

LEVELS

The construction of the levels can either be brickwork fashion, where the segments overlap each other by one-third, or stave construction, where the segments are in line. The segments will need support so a thin, solid intermediate ring is used to hold the open segments in line, as seen in the Skeleton Candlesticks project.

A variation on this theme is used in the Open-segment Flower Vase project (page 137), where a narrow intermediate solid segment is used to give the effect of a stave construction, and is removed after turning.

The ideal level thickness is ⁹⁄₁₆in (15mm). The thickness of the thinner intermediate segments can be as little as ¹⁄₁₆in (1mm) but ¹⁄₈in (3mm) works better. Segments with a thickness above ⁹⁄₁₆in (15mm) do tend to look like blocks of wood. The elegance of the design can easily be lost, but it all depends on the size of the object being produced.

With brickwork levels allow one-third of a segment overlap.

A narrow intermediate solid segment can be used during construction then removed.

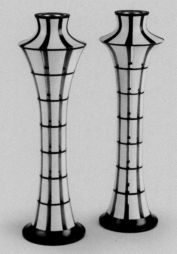

A thin, solid intermediate ring holds stave-construction segments in line.

This vessel was made from 2in (50mm) square blocks.

CLOSED SEGMENT TOP LEVEL

The design is always best closed off with a solid top, made either from a solid piece of wood or a solid-segment ring, and comprising the same number of segments as the open-segment rings so that the joins overlap. Depending on the design it does not always follow that the top ring has to be the same thickness as the open-segment rings.

TIP: If a closed-segment ring is being used following open-segment construction, do not forget to alter the mitre angle of the mitre saw.

Often a more elegant design can be created with a thinner top ring.

BUILDING UP THE OPEN-SEGMENT COMPOSITE

The segments are cut as for closed-segment construction, then the edges are either sanded on the disc sander or smoothed by using a very accurate and sharp mitre saw.

Gluing open segments needs a lot of care, not only to ensure that the segments are glued securely but also in removing any excess glue, as seen in the photo sequence.

You will need pipe cleaners, glue, glue brushes and a jar of cold water to soak them in between glue-ups.

1 Position the segments in the template. As in closed-segment construction, take care to ensure that grain direction is uniform.

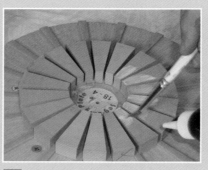

2 Apply glue to the segment edges using small paintbrushes.

3 Push the segments into the centre of the template to ensure that they are held firmly. If the diameter permits, fit a rubber band around the outside of the segments to hold them in place when mounting them on the lathe.

4 Before gluing the first level to the base, ensure the base is flat and sanded as it will be seen through the gaps.

> **TIP:** Choose a fast-acting PVA that will dry clear. Because there are no end-grain joints to be glued in the open segment stage, this adhesive is strong enough.

5 Now apply glue to the solid bottom face.

6 Mount the template on the tailstock and bring up to the headstock.

7 Push each segment firmly onto the base to ensure the glued surfaces are all in contact.

8 Use wet pipe cleaners to remove any excess glue.

9 Allow the segments to dry for at least eight hours. Level the faces with 120-grit sandpaper before gluing the next level. Before sanding, mark concentric circles on the segments with a pencil.

10 Using a piece of sandpaper in front of a backplate, sand the disc by hand or at a very slow lathe speed, taking care when applying pressure to ensure against vibration because that would break the segments. Uneven segments will show up after sanding. Repeat sanding until all the pencil lines have been removed.

11 Carefully paint the glue on with a fine artist's brush.

12 Fit the next level of segments to the template, glued and sandwiched brickwork fashion on the lathe as before.

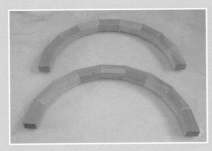

13 Glue up each level, leaving eight hours between each for the glue to cure, until completion of composite levels.

14 Usually the top level is made from a solid segment ring. The segments are cut and glued together in semi-circles with an aliphatic resin glue, as described in solid-segment techniques on page 55. It is usual to have the same number of segments in the solid ring as the open-segment levels, but the mitre angle will of course change. No allowance will be needed for the open gap.

15 When the glue has cured, true up the semi-circles and glue them together as a circle, then when dry sand the circle in a drum sander.

16 After ensuring that the open-segment levels are flat and true, glue the solid ring in situ on the lathe and remove any excess glue with wet pipe cleaners.

Turning the composite

Turning open-segment objects obviously requires a little more care than closed-segment objects. The techniques are fairly similar and the sequence of turning remains the same: the inside is turned first, the composite is then reverse chucked, and supported by the tailstock, to turn the outside. Before starting on the inside, remove the sharp edges on the outside to balance the composite on the lathe, enabling reasonably high turning speeds of 1000–1500rpm, dependent on the size of the composite. It is unwise to reach those speeds until the composite is balanced.

Supporting the composite

Normal open-segment composites mounted on a headstock faceplate do not require additional support. However, taller vessels may require support at various stages of their construction to allow the inside to be drilled out or turned. Sometimes the structure will either be too tall or the inside too tight to turn when the composite is completely built.

Normal composites do not require additional support.

A three-point steady is used for supporting some composites.

The Skeleton Candlesticks (page 155) will need supporting to hollow out the inside before the solid top is turned.

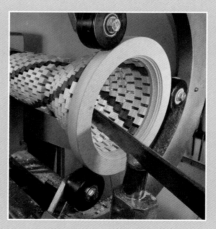

The Gherkin Lamp Stand (page 147) is made from two composites joined together.

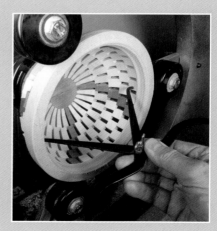

Both structures will need to be supported in a bowl steady before hollowing the insides.

Ample allowance needs to be made in the wall thickness of the lower levels of the composite to ensure stability when turning the inside.

It's best to glue a salvage piece of MDF to the top layers to act as the track for the lathe steady; the bare open-segment structure with its gaps would not be suitable. Once the inside has been hollowed out to the required shape the sacrificial MDF can be cut away ready for gluing the next level.

Turning the inside

The reverse-chucking technique requires the shape of the vessel to be created from the inside, whereas in conventional bowl turning the vessel shape is created from the outside. Depending on the wall thickness, it may be impossible owing to the instability of the structure to adjust the inside shape after the outside thickness has been reduced.

Using hollowing tools

The fastest way to remove the rough edges and get the inside of the composite down to size is with a hollowing tool. These usually have a limiter for the depth of cut, and this is set initially to a medium cut for edge removal and then to a finer cut to establish the contours.

Care must be taken with these tools as they can remove a lot of material very quickly, so start with a smaller gap to test the cut of the tool. This will vary according to the timber being used.

Go easy, starting with a smaller gap to test the tool's cut.

Using tungsten-tipped tools

A tungsten-tipped shear scraper makes much lighter work of turning the inside of an open-segmented vessel. These tools are available in a wide variety of sizes and tips. They are held at 45° and many have 45° flats on the shank for ease of control. Tungsten-tipped tools are ideal for turning plastics and Corian.

TIP: Some of the shear scrapers are supplied with HSS tips, which in many cases can be upgraded to Carbide tips, which are harder.

Many tungsten-tipped tools have 45° flats on the back for ease of control.

Teardrop shear scraping

The teardrop scraper is the ideal tool for finishing off the inside of the composite structure. The tool is held at a 45° angle to the work, with contact at the centre or slightly below centre of the composite.

The teardrop cutter will require frequent repositioning for the changing angles inside the composite. The edge quickly gets dull and will require much honing or grinding. The best results are a 90° grind on both top and bottom edges. The tool can then be quickly reversed to use both edges rather than keep grinding the one edge. A teardrop shear scraper will be used for finishing off the contour.

Holding the tool at 45° to the work.

Turning the outside

As the top of the composite vessel is turned to almost finished thickness it will start to vibrate. Segmenters traditionally supported the rim with their fingers to stop this vibration, but there is an easier way – to reverse chuck the composite.

By remounting the composite with the base supported by the tailstock and the top of the vessel supported in the headstock using a jam chuck, the whole composite can be supported and the walls taken down to the required thickness without any danger or vibration.

Once the inside has been turned the composite can be reverse-chucked.

Reversing the composite

I made a large cone out of MDF discs glued together, mounted on a wooden faceplate for my chuck and then turned. The MDF is soft enough not to mark the composite rim and provides enough bite to ensure it does not slip. Occasionally the face of the cone needs cleaning up to remove ridges that gradually build up.

When repositioning the composite care has to be taken to ensure that the base revolves centrally around the tailstock. I prefer to pre-drill the base of my wooden faceplate to fit the outside of the tailstock revolving centre so that they are always centred.

The cone face will need ridges removed from time to time.

Pre-drilling the faceplate base to fit the outside of the tailstock revolving centre ensures that it is central.

SHEAR-SCRAPING WITH THE BOWL GOUGE

Now that the ends are supported, the walls can be brought down to the finished thickness using the bowl gouge in shear-scraping mode.

A long slow sweep from the base to the centre works very well; then sweep from the rim to the centre to achieve the full effect.

Gradually reposition the edge of the bowl gouge from horizontal to almost vertical so the final shavings are fine twirls. You will be surprised how thin the walls can be taken down in size; I regularly have a finished thickness of below ⅛in (3mm) and some have been even thinner – not always intentionally.

Some segmenters use a bowl gouge with a swept-back fingernail grind for the internal surfaces, but I prefer tungsten-tipped tools for the inside.

1 As with solid segment construction the bowl gouge is used for turning the outside of the open segment composite – not in conventional bevel-rubbing mode, but in shear-scraping mode.

2 The bowl gouge can be used for both roughing and final finishing of the outside of the open-segmented composite.

3 The top outside rim is then brought down to size using the bowl gouge in shear-scraping mode.

4 The base is then brought down to approximate size. It will be removed from the faceplate later for final finishing.

5 Initially, the gouge is held horizontally to the toolrest; later, for the finishing cut, the edge is held almost vertically. When held vertically the edge puts no stress at all on the composite and fine twirly shavings are created. This technique is ideal for the finishing cuts of very fine structures.

6 The left-hand shavings are normal roughing shear cuts, the centre group is light shear shavings and the right-hand shavings are those produced with the gouge cutting edge almost vertical.

NEGATIVE-RAKE SCRAPER

A negative-rake scraper can be placed flat on the toolrest instead of at a 45° angle, which is the shear-scraping mode. The negative bevel on the top edge ensures that the tool will not dig in. The bevel still slopes towards the wood, but the burr created where the two bevels intersect will still cut the wood. Many of us have used a skew gouge flat on its side on the toolrest to finish off a surface; that is in effect a negative-rake scraper. It is used for finishing cuts.

These scrapers can be used both inside and outside the composite. I have a long bar scraper with the cutting edge down its side that allows it to be used in deep vessels like candlesticks and flutes. I have flat and round scrapers, also with a negative rake, for use on the outside of the composite. They are the main tools used for finishing plastics and Corian.

The negative-rake side scraper is great for cleaning up the insides of candlesticks.

FINISHING THE BASE

With the wooden backing plate attached to the base it is not always easy to finish off the outside of the base. Best results are achieved by sanding the piece, then taking it off the lathe to inspect it before final separation. Its shape cannot be changed once it has been separated from the backing plate. Use of the paper glue joint makes separation easy.

The finished composite is then remounted on the lathe in reverse jam chuck mode and the base supported by a drive centre. I use a small stebcentre to support the base in the tailstock – it hardly marks the base, which is not a problem because the centre pip will be removed later.

The base is then cleaned up and slightly undercut to enable it to sit correctly.

The pip is removed after sanding and finishing and is best done with gentle cuts from a woodcarving gouge. The base can then be sanded using 120 grit working up to 400 grit.

A stebcentre supports the base in the tailstock.

Undercut the base with a spindle gouge.

The centre pip will be removed later.

FINISHING

Care has to be taken when finishing an open-segment composite. It is best to de-nib the segment edges before sanding; whiskers will be seen growing out of some of the cut edges, held on by the flexible glue. These are easily removed using a needle file; be careful not to mark these sharp edges with the file. A tapered triangular needle file is good for getting into the corners if there is any slight glue residue; a square file will leave edge marks.

A tapered triangular needle file removes glue from corners whereas a square file leaves edge marks.

LACQUERS

Conventional oils and wood finishes are not ideal for open segments especially if they have to be applied with a brush or a cloth. The most satisfactory finish is spray lacquer. Start with a sanding sealer; when dry de-nib the vessel with an abrasive pad and then apply three coats of finished lacquer, again de-nibbing with a fine abrasive pad between each coat. An abrasive pad is better than wire wool for de-nibbing because wire wool can easily get caught between the segments.

Leave at least four hours between coats; the lacquer may look dry but it is easily marked with the abrasive pad if it is not hard enough.

SANDING

If the sandpaper is not held flat when sanding the composite, and the speed of rotation kept at about 100rpm, the edges of the segments will get rounded off. A flat rotating sanding disc either fitted to a handle or to an electric drill works well.

Depending on the type of wood used and the finish already achieved by turning, start with 180 grit and work up to 400. Once the piece has been sanded inspect the segments – if there are still some tool marks or coarse-grade sandpaper marks, then the process should be repeated until they are removed.

Mirka Abranet abrasives work exceptionally well as they have an open texture that allows resinous dust to escape from the surface and be extracted so clogging cannot occur. They work long after other abrasives have given up.

EBONIZING

An alternative to clear lacquer is ebonizing lacquer. This is used in the Open-segment Candlesticks project to pleasing effect. Two coats will be needed after using the sanding sealer and then finished with one or two coats of the clear lacquer finish.

Repeat the sanding process until tool marks are removed.

The finished composite should look like this.

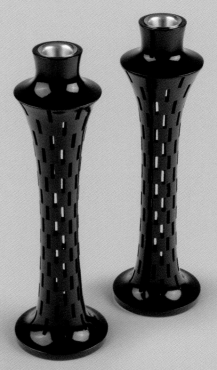

An ebonized finish should look like this.

THE PROJECTS

SEGMENTED BOWL

This first project shows you how to create a simple segmented
bowl with a few tools and basic equipment. Any planed hardwood
decking plank would be fine for this project. I used ¹/₂in (13mm)
ipe *(Tabebuia spp.)* decking, available at most DIY stores. An oily
wood the colour of walnut, it is straight grained and easy to turn.
The thickness is not critical as long as it is uniform. You will also
need a length of beading, shown here in ramin *(Gonystylus spp.)*.
The bowl takes about three hours to make, but in stages spread
over a week to allow for the adhesive and finish to dry.

Skill level:
● **Beginner**

SEGMENTED BOWL

YOU WILL NEED:

EQUIPMENT
Circular saw
Mitre saw
Lathe
Bandsaw
Disc sander

MATERIALS
Ipe (*Tabebuia spp.*) – 6ft (2m) length
of planed decking x ½in x 5¼in
(13 x 135mm)
Ramin (*Gonystylus spp.*) – 6ft (2m)
length of planed beading x 1 x ⅛in
(25 x 3mm)

TOOLS
⅝in (16mm) bowl gouge
¾in (19mm) half-round scraper
Teardrop scraper

DESIGN

This is a simple design with a solid base plus six layers with 12 segments per layer at 30°, which need a 15° mitre angle. These have been created using the Woodturner Studio CAD program. Since the decking is already planed, it can be cut into strips on the circular saw to the widths shown for each segment level. The dimensions are not critical as long as they are larger than shown on the cutting list.

Block diagram

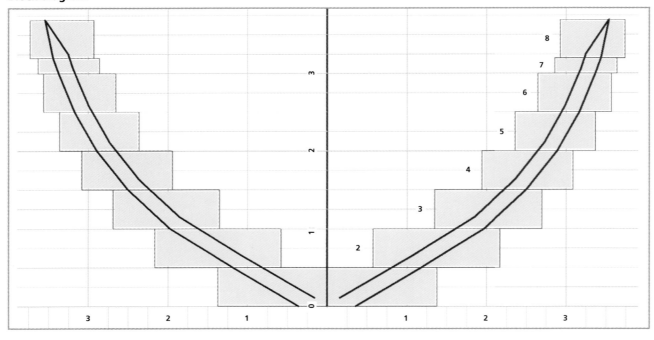

Cutting list

Layer no.	No. of segments		Outer radius	Inner radius	Length	Width	Mitre angle	Gap angle	Vessel radius	Board thickness	Board length	Edge radius
Base			Solid layer 2.554 diameter x 0.500 thickness									
2	12		2.172	0.574	1.164	1.599	15.000	0.000	1.972	0.500	11.950	2.249
3	12		2.700	1.349	1.447	1.351	15.000	0.000	2.500	0.500	16.074	2.796
4	12		3.086	1.941	1.654	1.145	15.000	0.000	2.886	0.500	19.162	3.195
5	12		3.368	2.350	1.805	1.017	15.000	0.000	3.168	0.500	21.351	3.487
6	12		3.574	2.645	1.915	0.929	15.000	0.000	3.374	0.500	22.936	3.700
7	12		3.638	2.857	1.950	0.782	15.000	0.000	3.438	0.200	23.785	3.767
Top	12		3.735	2.925	2.002	0.811	15.000	0.000	3.535	0.500	24.325	3.867

Measurements are in inches

Section view

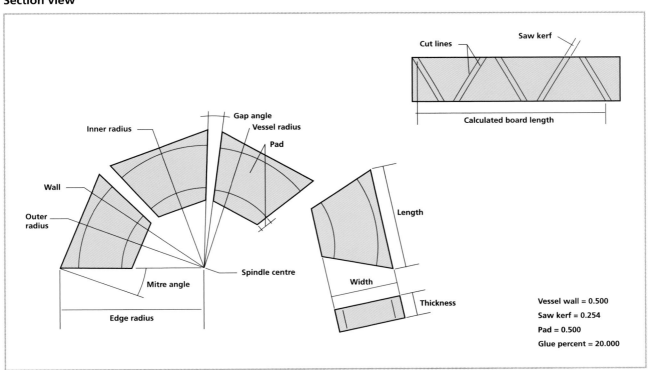

Vessel wall = 0.500
Saw kerf = 0.254
Pad = 0.500
Glue percent = 20.000

CUTTING AND CONSTRUCTION

1 Begin by cutting the solid base of the bowl. Trim the edges of the square piece of timber by hand or on a bandsaw to make life easier when turning.

2 Glue the base onto a wooden faceplate, which has been already set up to fit the chuck jaws; this saves wood and gives more room to part off when finishing the piece. By using a paper joint it can be easily separated later without reducing the thickness of the base.

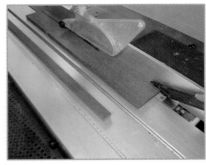

3 Cut the segment lengths. It is best to cut them all at the same time.

SAFETY ADVICE: When cutting the segment lengths, take care to use a push-stick as circular saws are very dangerous.

4 Now cut the segments on the mitre saw. A dummy wooden backplate added to the mitre saw will stop the segments flying off; an end stop will gauge the segment lengths. Set the mitre saw to 15°.

SAFETY ADVICE: Remember to keep your fingers well out of the way when using the mitre saw.

5 Obtain a very clean cut by slowly lowering the spinning blade onto the wood.

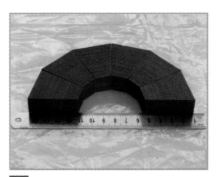

6 It it is a good idea to cut six segments (a semi-circle) from scrap wood to check the mitre angle.

7 Clean off any burr on the edges of the segments ready for gluing them together. Line them up to arrange the grain direction before gluing up.

8 A yellow aliphatic glue, such as Titebond, is best for gluing end grain.

9 Rub the segments together, hold them in position and then, after a couple of seconds, the glue will grab.

TIP: I glue the segments on a sheet of polythene placed on a thick piece of glass, but any flat surface will do.

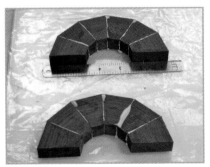

10 Once a semi-circle of segments has been glued up, check the segment alignment with a rule.

11 When the half rings are dry, clean up on the drum sander or a flat piece of sandpaper.

12 Align the edges using the drum sander or with sandpaper.

14 Glue the two half rings together on a flat surface.

13 Once sanded, piece together to check that everything is correct.

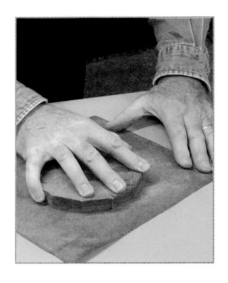

15 Clean away any glue residue on the sides of the first level by rubbing them, under pressure, on 80-grit sandpaper.

16 Now glue up the first level and position on the lathe between the base and the backplate. When it is centred, adjust the tailstock to clamp the levels finger tight.

17 Once the glue has dried (usually after eight hours), true and flatten the level with sandpaper. Use a sheet of 120-grit paper to flatten the segment ring.

18 Now gradually build up the levels, aligning the segments brickwork fashion as you progress.

19 True up each level before gluing the next one and build it up to the required level.

20 To add a bit of interest, a ramin feature-ring is included in the design. Construct this 12-segment ring as you did for the other rings. Complete all the levels and the finished composite bowl should look something like this.

TIP: It may be better to cut the thin segments on a bandsaw, as smaller pieces tend to fly off when cut on a mitre saw.

TURNING

21 Now for the exciting bit – creating your own beautiful bowl from the composite made from a plank of wood. First, the outside must be cleaned up, as those sharp edges are dangerous.

22 Remove the outer edges using the bowl gouge on its side in shear-scraping mode (see page 61).

23 When the outside edges have been removed, but not the thickness of the wall, the composite should look like this.

24 The inside can now be turned while there is adequate support in the bowl wall thickness. Remove the rough edges on the inside using a scraper on its side at approximately 45°; this is known as shear scraping (see page 59). Take light cuts initially at a medium speed (500rpm) until the segment edges are eliminated.

25 Once the inside is smooth, use the teardrop scraper to create a smooth contour. Again it is presented at a 45° angle to the wood. Increase the lathe speed to 1,000rpm to enable delicate whispers of shavings to be made.

26 Once the inside has been turned it can be sanded with a sanding disc. Start at 120 grit and work up to 400 grit. Small tears in the grain on the inside can be quickly eliminated with some sanding treatment.

27 The outside can now be finished. Reverse the bowl on the chuck, with the top edge supported by a jam chuck made from MDF (see page 62).

28 Support the bottom of the bowl on the tailstock using the centre of the faceplate.

29 Bring the top of the outside of the bowl down to finished size using the bowl gouge in shear-scraping mode. The base cannot be turned to finished size at this stage, as the faceplate will get in the way.

30 Once you are happy with the top, make a start on the lower half. The bowl now needs to be broken away from its faceplate using a sharp knife.

31 Remount the bowl on the MDF jam chuck, with the base supported by a small stebcentre. Care needs to be taken to ensure the base is running true, so adjust the stebcentre's point of contact. Once it is running true it can be tightened up.

32 Smooth out the edges of the lower levels and create the foot of the base using the bowl gouge in shear-scraping mode.

33 Create the final bowl shape by taking long sweeping strokes with the bowl gouge to give a smooth outline.

34 Hollow and true the underside of the base using the half-round scraper at 45°. Hollow the base so that the bowl sits on the base edge.

FINISHING

35 Sand the bowl with a 2in (50mm) sanding disc, starting at 120 grit and working up to 400 grit.

36 Take the bowl from the lathe and remove the pip with a carving chisel.

37 Sand the area to a smooth finish.

38 Finish the bowl with one coat of sanding sealer and three coats of acrylic satin lacquer. Allow a couple of hours between coats for the finish to harden, then de-nib with an abrasive pad between coats to remove fibres and dust. The finished bowl should look something like this.

BASIC ORNATE BOWL

Ornate segmented bowls are very popular in America and are
starting to appear at exhibitions in the UK. There are many books
on the subject of laminations and some very complicated designs.
This project uses different woods and segment thicknesses to
create a simple laminated feature. Beech *(Fagus sylvatica)* has
been used as the main white wood and mahogany *(Maliaceae)*
as the contrasting darker wood, but any contrasting hardwoods
would do, such as ash *(Fraxinus spp)*, maple *(Acer spp.)*, ebony
(Diospyros spp.) or blackwood *(Dalbergia spp.)*. The thickness is
not critical as long as it is uniform. The bowl takes approximately
four hours to make, but in stages spread over a week to allow for
the adhesive and finish to dry.

BASIC ORNATE BOWL

YOU WILL NEED:

EQUIPMENT

Circular saw
Planer thicknesser
Mitre saw
Lathe
Drum sander
Bandsaw
Disc sander

MATERIALS

Mahogany (*Maliaceae*) – 1 piece
3¼ x ½ x 28½in (85 x 13 x 723mm)
Beech (*Fagus sylvatica*) – 3 pieces
3¼ x ½ x 25½in (85 x 13 x 650mm)
Yellow aliphatic glue
Sealer
Acrylic satin lacquer

TOOLS

⅝in (16mm) bowl gouge
Tungsten-tipped shear scraper
Teardrop scraper
Hollowing tool
Callipers

DESIGN

This design was developed using the Woodturner Studio CAD program. It is an eight-layer design with 18 segments per layer of 20°, which require a 10° mitre angle. Most of the levels are ½in (13mm) thickness but the top layer is ⅜in (10mm). The laminated feature ring was developed using beech and mahogany segments.

Block diagram

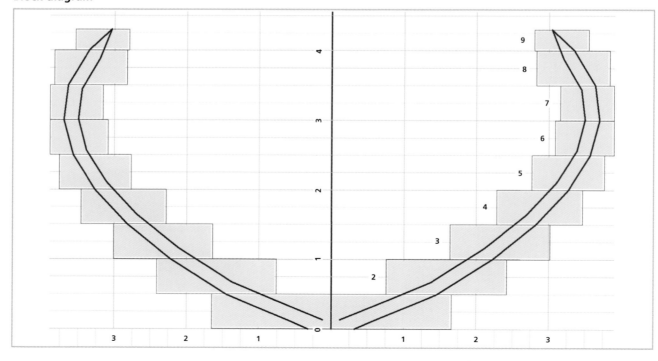

Cutting list

Layer no.	No. of segments		Outer radius	Inner radius	Length	Width	Mitre angle	Gap angle	Vessel radius	Board thickness	Board length	Edge radius
Base			Solid layer 3.111 diameter x 0.500 thickness									
2	18		2.420	0.748	0.853	1.672	10.000	0.000	2.220	0.500	14.208	2.457
3	18		3.021	1.630	1.065	1.391	10.000	0.000	2.821	0.500	18.864	3.068
4	18		3.472	2.273	1.224	1.199	10.000	0.000	3.272	0.500	22.305	3.526
5	18		3.767	2.760	1.329	1.007	10.000	0.000	3.567	0.500	24.753	3.825
6	18	12 6	3.898	3.087	1.375	0.811	10.000	0.000	3.698	0.500	26.174	3.959
7	18	12 6	3.898	3.158	1.375	0.741	10.000	0.000	3.698	0.500	26.384	3.959
8	18		3.837	2.818	1.353	1.020	10.000	0.000	3.637	0.500	25.162	3.897
Top	18		3.547	2.601	1.251	0.946	10.000	0.000	3.347	0.300	23.538	3.602

Measurements are in inches

Section view

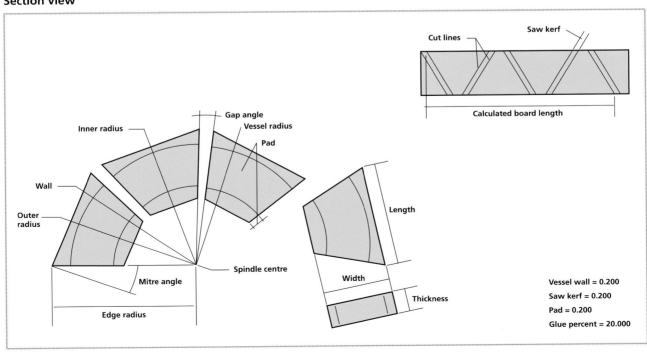

Cut lines
Saw kerf
Calculated board length

Inner radius
Gap angle
Vessel radius
Pad
Wall
Outer radius
Spindle centre
Mitre angle
Edge radius
Length
Width
Thickness

Vessel wall = 0.200
Saw kerf = 0.200
Pad = 0.200
Glue percent = 20.000

CUTTING AND CONSTRUCTION

1 Since the levels are of varying thickness the first stage is to cut the wood into the appropriate strips on the circular saw.

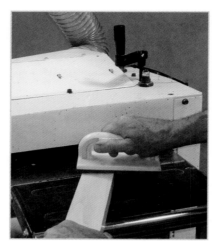

2 Plane the strips, ideally using a thicknesser to achieve uniform thickness, then cut them to the appropriate width on the circular saw. The dimensions are not critical as long as they are larger than shown on the cutting list. However, it is best to be as accurate as possible on the feature ring to maintain the pattern – the ½in (13mm) verticals are the same width as the horizontals.

3 Cut the segments on the mitre saw. The mitre saw should be set to 10°. A very clean cut can be obtained by slowly lowering the spinning blade onto the wood.

4 It may be worth cutting nine segments (a semi-circle) using scrap wood to check the mitre angle.

SAFETY ADVICE: Cutting the thin ⅜in (10mm) mahogany strip on the mitre saw is a little dangerous, as the thin segments can fly out, so I used a bandsaw to cut this strip.

SAFETY ADVICE: Remember to keep your fingers well out of the way when using the mitre saw.

5 Arrange the segments before gluing to ensure that their grain pattern runs in the same direction.

TIP: As the accuracy of the joint is important on delicate objects, I clean up the mahogany segments on a disc sander to ensure that the angle is correct, but you can get away with sawn edges.

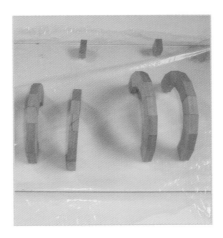

6 Clean off any burr on the edges, then glue the segments together in half circles.

7 After about 20 minutes stand the segments up to allow the glue to dry on all surfaces.

8 The feature ring segments comprise two dark wooden segments next to one white one. Just be careful the two semi-circles will match when joined together.

9 True up the semi-circle faces on the disc sander before the two halves are glued together.

10 Remove the excess glue from the two surfaces and then true up the mitre face.

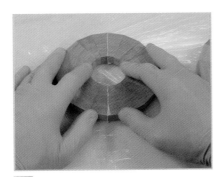

11 Glue the half circles together to form the rings.

12 When the glue is dry, sand the completed levels in a drum sander to remove the excess glue and sort out any slight segment misalignments; this could also be done by hand on a sheet of sandpaper.

13 The bottom of the bowl is solid. Start by gluing the base to a wooden faceplate. Using a paper glue joint saves wood and provides a simple way to part off when finishing the piece.

14 In order to centralize the levels during glue-up on the lathe, use an MDF backplate with concentric circles drawn on it to aid alignment of the levels; you can also line them up by eye. Glue up the first level and position it on the lathe between the base and the backplate. When it is centred, adjust the tailstock to clamp the levels finger tight.

15 Once the glue has dried (usually after eight hours) true up the composite face using a bowl gouge on its side, shear-scraper fashion, and check for accuracy with a metal rule.

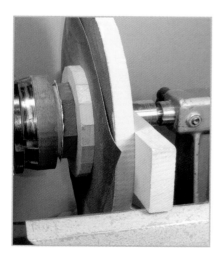

16 Sand the composite face flat using a piece of sandpaper between the bowl and the MDF backplate. If you are not able to select a very slow speed on the lathe, then this sanding should be undertaken manually by rotating the headstock by hand and holding the backplate stationary.

17 Gradually build up the levels of the composite, aligning the segments brickwork fashion. True up each level before gluing the next.

18 Check that the alignment is correct when gluing together the two feature-ring levels.

19 Complete all the levels and the finished composite bowl should look something like this.

TURNING

20 Before turning the composite down to size, remove the rough edges from the outside of the bowl, using the bowl gouge on its side in shear-scraping mode.

21 Cut the edges back but do not reduce the wall thickness at this stage.

22 Now remove the rough edges on the inside using a hollowing tool to eliminate the excess. Take light cuts initially at a medium speed until the segment edges are gone.

23 The hollowing tool will tear the wood, so opt for a tungsten-tipped shear scraper to bring the inside down to just above the final dimension.

24 Once the inside is almost to its finished dimension, use a teardrop scraper to create a smooth contour from the bottom to the sides of the bowl.

25 Stop the lathe and use light finger pressure to check the internal contour for tool marks and flats.

26 Use a side-cutting tungsten-tipped scraper for the internal part of the top and the rim. Again these scrapers are presented at a 45° angle to the wood.

27 The outside can now be cleaned up. Reverse the bowl onto a jam chuck made from a cone built up from MDF. Centre the base on the tailstock centre until the bowl runs true.

28 Use the bowl gouge on its side in shear-scraping mode to achieve a clean cut without undue stress on the bowl. Start at the top half of the bowl to obtain the desired shape. You can still go back to the inside at this stage if the shape is not right, but you cannot go back to the top once you start to reduce the thickness from the lower half of the bowl.

29 Check the wall thickness either by hand or with callipers and reposition the composite on the lathe for removal of any high spots.

30 Once you are happy with the top, start on the lower half. First, smooth out the edges of the lower levels, then start to shape the base.

31 The faceplate may start to get in the way, so it can now be removed by splitting the paper joint with a sharp knife.

32 Reposition the composite on the lathe. Use of a small stebcentre allows, by trial and error, repositioning of the centre without indentation of the base.

33 Hollow the base to ensure it stands without rocking and establish the outside shape with the bowl gouge. Now form the base and lower half by taking long sweeping strokes to give a smooth outline.

FINISHING

34 Sand the bowl with an electric drill fitted with a 2in (50mm) sanding disc. Start at 120 grit and work up to 400 grit. Finish sanding the exterior, then remove the bowl from the lathe and finish off the base by using a hand chisel to take off the stub left by the stebcentre. Sand to your satisfaction.

35 To avoid the dark wood colour leeching into the white wood, try out your proposed finish on some scrap pieces first. Some sanding sealers do make the colours run. Acrylic lacquer works well but put on a sealer base coat first. Apply three coats of clear acrylic satin lacquer. After each coat is dry, burnish the bowl with either wire wool or an abrasive pad to remove any raised fibres and dust. The finished result should look something like this.

OPEN-SEGMENT FRUIT BOWL

In this project we will make a simple open-segment fruit bowl using a SegEasy template. This bowl is made from whitebeam *(Sorbus spp.)* that was planked and dried from a tree in my garden. It is a pale cream hardwood that is stable and turns very well. Due to the fragile nature of construction, the wood has to be extremely dry, otherwise, after the bowl has been built, movement through drying will cause the segments to crack. The bowl takes approximately four hours to make, but in stages spread over a week to allow for the adhesive and finish to dry.

Skill level:
● **Beginner**

OPEN-SEGMENT FRUIT BOWL

YOU WILL NEED:

EQUIPMENT
Circular saw
Planer thicknesser
Mitre saw
Lathe
Drum sander
Disc sander

MATERIALS
Whitebeam *(Sorbus spp.)*
White PVA
Yellow aliphatic glue
Acrylic satin lacquer

TOOLS
⅝in (16mm) bowl gouge
Tungsten-tipped shear scraper
or ring tool
Teardrop scraper
Hollowing tool

DESIGN

For this project we use an 18-segment SegEasy template which is mounted onto several layers of MDF for rigidity. The template has a small centre hole that allows you to drill through the MDF to provide an accurate means of centring the plate on tailstock.

The SegEasy plate uses a 4° angle which gives a 20° segment with an 8° mitre angle. The open-segment bowl is an eight-layer design with 18 segments per layer. The base is solid and the top level is an 18-piece closed-segment ring with a 10° mitre angle.

The levels are all ½in (13mm) thickness except for the top level, which is ⅜in (10mm) thick. The design was developed on the Woodturner Studio CAD program, which automatically handles closed- and open-segment design with varying segment angles.

Block diagram

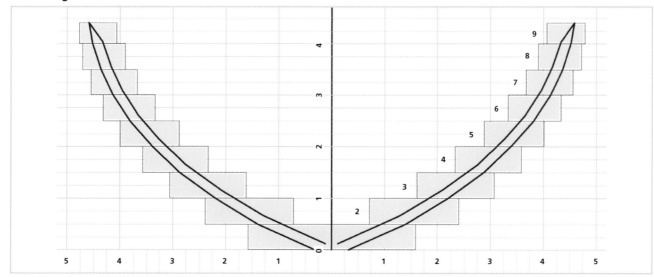

Cutting list

Layer no.	No. of segments		Outer radius	Inner radius	Length	Width	Mitre angle	Gap angle	Vessel radius	Board thickness	Board Length	Edge Radius
Base			Solid layer 2.963 diameter x 0.500 thickness									
2	18		2.401	0.705	0.675	1.696	8.000	4.000	2.201	0.500	11.934	2.425
3	18		3.064	1.601	0.861	1.463	8.000	4.000	2.864	0.500	15.845	3.094
4	18		3.593	2.309	1.010	1.284	8.000	4.000	3.393	0.500	18.949	3.629
5	18		4.011	2.874	1.127	1.137	8.000	4.000	3.811	0.500	21.414	4.051
6	18		4.330	3.318	1.217	1.012	8.000	4.000	4.130	0.500	23.327	4.373
7	18		4.563	3.657	1.283	0.907	8.000	4.000	4.363	0.500	24.760	4.608
8	18		4.717	3.904	1.326	0.812	8.000	4.000	4.517	0.500	25.761	4.763
Top	18		4.784	4.045	1.687	0.739	10.000	0.000	4.584	0.400	32.013	4.858

Measurements are in inches

Section view

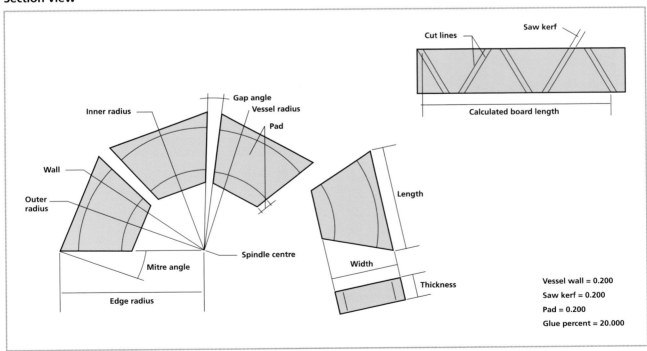

Vessel wall = 0.200
Saw kerf = 0.200
Pad = 0.200
Glue percent = 20.000

CUTTING AND CONSTRUCTION

1 First, cut the wood into the appropriate strips on the circular saw and then plane to thickness – ideally using a thicknesser for uniformity. Now size to the appropriate width on the circular saw and plane the sawn face. Next, cut the segments on the mitre saw set to an 8° mitre angle with a new false backplate to give an accurate cut.

TIP: The thickness of the strips must be consistent, as there is little room to handle discrepancies in the thickness of the segments during the build-up.

2 The bottom of the bowl is solid. Start by gluing the base to a wooden faceplate. Use a paper glue joint, and before gluing ensure that both surfaces are flat.

3 Clean off any burr on the edges of the segments with a warding file, then assemble the segments on the template. Make sure that the grain direction is consistent.

4 Using a glue brush, glue the segments onto the template and the base level onto the lathe.

TIP: For open-segment work I use white PVA glue. Any excess glue contracts and almost seems to disappear. This glue is not as strong as the aliphatic yellow glues on end grain. However, on side grain, which is the main area that is glued in open-segment work, it is stronger than the wood itself. Yellow aliphatic glue leaves a dark yellow glue line when it dries, so for this reason too white PVA is preferable.

5 Glue up the first level and position it on the lathe between the base and the template so that it is centred on the tailstock. After positioning, adjust the levels to be finger tight.

6 Remove the excess glue from between the segments using pipe cleaners soaked in water. Place the pipe cleaners back into the water afterwards and the glue will dissolve so they can be used again.

7 Once the glue has dried, the next level can be constructed.

8 In order to ensure the segments are all the same height, sand the glued-up level on the lathe using 120-grit paper wedged between the level and a large MDF backplate.

9 Scribble pencil lines on each segment before sanding and keep sanding until all the pencil lines disappear.

TIP: For sanding the segments level, the lathe speed needs to be very slow, with hardly any pressure from the tailstock, otherwise the segments will break away. If your lathe does not have speed control then manually turn the composite structure against the sandpaper.

10 As the segment size increases the glue can be applied just to the edges; this saves cleaning away excess glue later.

11 Line up the segment levels in a brickwork fashion. Push the segments firmly down into the template because some of them may have moved while they were being positioned on the lathe.

12 Make sure the excess glue is removed at each stage.

13 Remove excess glue using pipe cleaners. Leave to dry.

14 The final level is made using a closed-segment ring. The segments are cut on the mitre saw set to 10°. Construct the level by gluing up two semi-circles with yellow aliphatic glue.

15 When the glue is dry, align the two halves and glue them together. After eight hours, sand the completed ring in a drum sander to remove the excess glue and sort out any slight segment misalignments, or do this by hand on a sheet of sandpaper.

16 Glue the top level of open segments and the corresponding closed-segment ring with white PVA glue. Align the levels on the lathe using an MDF backplate to apply pressure on the top level. Clear any excess glue using the pipe cleaners.

17 The finished composite bowl should look something like this.

TURNING

18 Open segments can quickly splinter so the interior sharp edges should first be removed using either a hollowing tool, which is quicker and easier to control, or a shear scraper.

19 Take light cuts initially at a medium speed until the segment edges are eliminated.

20 Once the inside shape has been roughed out it can be smoothed out using a shear scraper at 45° in a pull cut at medium speed or with a tungsten-tipped ring tool (see Step 21).

21 I prefer to use a tungsten-tipped ring tool, which gives a very precise cut without any chatter or vibration on the bowl edge in a pull cut at medium to high speed.

22 Once the inside is smooth, use the teardrop scraper to create a smooth contour for the bowl. Again the scraper should be presented at a 45° angle to the wood for a pull cut. The lathe can now be speeded up to enable delicate whiskers of shavings to be made.

23 Clean up the rim using either a bowl gouge on its side in shear-scraping mode or with the tungsten-tipped tool.

24 Since an open-segmented bowl does not have the rigidity of a normal bowl, it is better to reverse the bowl on the lathe using a jam chuck for rim support. But before reversing the bowl, the inside must be sanded. Using a 2in (50mm) sanding disc mounted on either an electric drill or an angle sander, start at 120 grit and gradually work up to 400 grit.

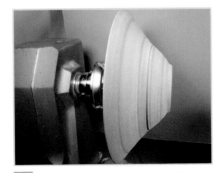

25 Jam chucks come in many shapes and sizes. I like a cone made up from concentric rings of MDF which can be used for all sizes of bowls.

26 Turn the bowl round and mount it on the MDF cone, then centre the faceplate base on the tailstock. The outside can now be cleaned up.

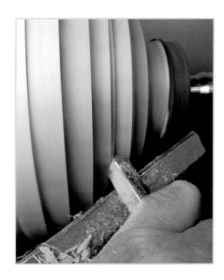

27 As with the inside, the rough edges can be more easily removed using the bowl gouge on its side in shear-scraping pull-mode. It gives a clean cut without undue stress on the bowl. Start by removing all the sharp edges to get the composite down to a round form.

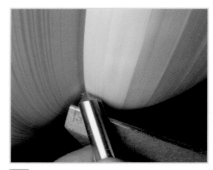

28 Carefully cut away the top half of the bowl to achieve the desired shape.

29 Once you are happy with the top, start on the lower half, first establishing the shape of the lower levels.

TIP: The great thing about open-segment work is that you can see the thickness of the bowl at any stage through the gaps. I like to achieve a wall thickness of a uniform ⅛in (3mm); it takes a strong nerve and a steady hand, but the effect is stunning. The wall thickness speaks a lot about the confidence of the turner.

30 To finish off the base of the bowl, it has to be removed from its faceplate. A paper glue joint is easily separated using a sharp knife and a gentle tap from a hammer, doing this off the lathe as the tap could damage your lathe bearings. I prefer to use router matting to support the faceplate.

31 Remount the bowl on the jam chuck using a small stebcentre on the tailstock.

32 The base can now be shaped and the bottom undercut to enable the base to stand without wobbling.

33 Finish off with a lathe speed of about 1,000 rpm and the bowl gouge at a 45° angle to shear scrape fine whiskers in long, sweeping pull strokes.

FINISHING

34 Sand the bowl as before, starting at 120 grit and working up to 400 grit. Clean up any small burrs from the segments using a needle file.

35 Once the outside has been sanded, the pip from the middle of the base can be removed with a carving chisel.

36 Sand the bottom of the base again through the grits from 120 to 400.

37 Acrylic lacquer spray works well but be careful of runs. Apply three coats of clear acrylic satin lacquer. After each coat is dry, burnish the bowl with either 400 grit sandpaper or an abrasive pad to remove any raised fibres and dust until the bowl looks like this. Do not use wire-wool for finishing, as it will get caught in the segments.

CORIAN BOWL

The design of the bowl uses a traditional concentric solid-ring approach. The bowl is made from just three squares of material with very little waste. I have chosen to use a man-made material: Corian. However, any material could be used with this technique – solid wood, man-made woods such as plywood, blockboard, laminaboard as well as plastics and stone.

CORIAN BOWL

YOU WILL NEED:

EQUIPMENT
Circular saw
Lathe
Disc sander

MATERIALS
Corian – 3 different-coloured squares
measuring 12in (305mm) square x
½in (13mm) thick
CA glue
Corian base adhesive

TOOLS
Tungsten-tipped shear scraper
Teardrop scraper
Flat negative-rake scraper
Callipers
Skew chisel
Parting tool

DESIGN

The easiest way to make a composite bowl out of Corian is to glue squares of sheet together in layers. The centres are cut out before construction.

By carefully designing the bowl, a minimum amount of Corian is used. The block diagram and cutting list denote a simple design based on

a flat-sided 55° conical bowl. Instead of eight separate squares of Corian, only three are used for this design, with the minimum of waste.

Block diagram

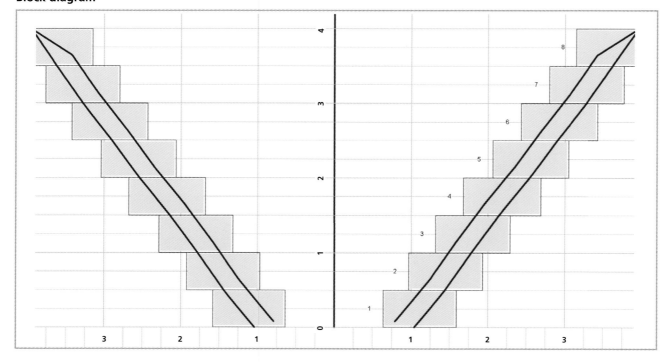

Cutting list

Layer no.	No. of segments	Outer radius	Inner radius	Length	Width	Mitre angle	Gap angle	Vessel radius	Board thickness	Board length	Edge radius
Base	☐ Solid layer 3.030 diameter x 0.500 thickness										
2	▬ Solid layer 3.710 diameter x 0.500 thickness										
3	▬ Solid layer 4.430 diameter x 0.500 thickness										
4	☐ Solid layer 5.230 diameter x 0.500 thickness										
5	▬ Solid layer 5.950 diameter x 0.500 thickness										
6	▬ Solid layer 6.710 diameter x 0.500 thickness										
7	☐ Solid layer 7.390 diameter x 0.500 thickness										
Top	▬ Solid layer 8.070 diameter x 0.500 thickness										

Measurements are in inches

Section view

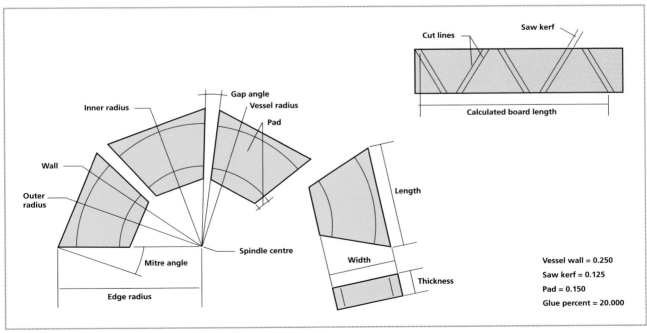

Vessel wall = 0.250
Saw kerf = 0.125
Pad = 0.150
Glue percent = 20.000

CUTTING AND CONSTRUCTION

1 Cut the sheet into squares using the circular saw fitted with a laminate tungsten-tipped fine-tooth blade to give a clean cut to the material.

2 Mount the squares on the lathe using large four-button jaws that work equally well on round and square objects. I use a metalwork lathe to cut the rings with a parting-off tool, but they can equally be cut to size on a wood lathe using a thin parting tool. A square of ³⁄₁₆in (5mm) hardboard is positioned behind the Corian to avoid the parting tool hitting the jaws.

3 To provide the maximum of material for turning later, it is better to cut at an angle. Shown here is the square being cutting at about 30°.

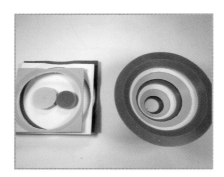

4 Cut each layer individually from the squares, starting at the smaller diameters and working outwards; this is a process that results in little waste.

5 Glue the Corian base to a wooden faceplate using thick CA glue. Only a small amount of glue is needed, the Corian base being spun on the faceplate to spread the glue evenly and then tightened with a large revolving stebcentre on the tailstock. Not a lot of pressure is needed. An activator spray can speed up the curing of the excess CA glue on the outside, but the inside can take up to two hours to cure properly.

SAFETY ADVICE: Always wear disposable gloves when using CA glue – fingers can become stuck all too easily! Allow for adequate ventilation.

6 Once the Corian base adhesive has set, the next layer can be similarly glued. Corian is highly polished and it is best to rub the surfaces with 120-grit sandpaper before gluing to give the adhesive a surface on which to bite. Position the layers using an MDF backplate with concentric circles drawn on it.

7 After each level has been glued it is good practice to clean up the composites by making sure the outside and inside are running concentrically. This action makes centring the next level easier.

8 Repeat the process for the remaining levels.

TURNING

9 After construction leave the composite for 24 hours to allow the CA glue to cure between the layers, then clean up the outside using a tungsten-tipped shear scraper. Finish is not important at this stage, so the lathe speed can be held at about 500rpm. At this speed the Corian splinters, enabling the material to be cut back quickly. A finishing cut will need a much slower speed to achieve those beautiful shavings.

10 Because of this bowl's very small base and thin side walls it is preferable to use a lathe steady to support the rim when turning the inside. Here, a flat has been made on the rim to accommodate the lathe-steady rollers without cutting into them. Rough down the inside to size using the tungsten-tipped shear scraper.

11 Once the final size is approached reduce lathe speed for a smoother cut, then achieve the final finish with a teardrop scraper.

12 After a fingertip check for bumps or dips, make any necessary adjustment.

13 Getting the top right is easy but you can still have a wide lower half, so use callipers to check side thickness.

14 Now reverse the bowl on the lathe to finish the outside. A cone made from MDF acts as a very good jam-chuck support for the rim. Start by using the tungsten-tipped scraper at a slow speed (200rpm) to clean up the outside.

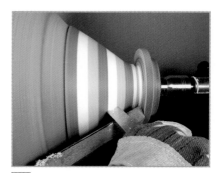

15 Clean up surface marks using the flat negative-rake scraper.

16 Before the bowl is parted off to finish the base, the inside must be sanded and polished, ideally using Mirka Abranet sanding pads because their open texture allows the dust to be removed without clogging. Start at 120 grit and work up to 1000 grit using a rotary sanding tool. You may have to keep going back to earlier grits to eliminate all the scratches. Remember there is no gloss finish – the finish is the sanded material.

17 When the inside has been polished, buff it with a sheepskin mop using a car polish such as Auto Glym.

18 The inside should shine with no visible scratches.

19 The bowl can now be parted off from the faceplate. It is easier to part off the wood and cut the final ½in (13mm) with a small saw.

FINISHING

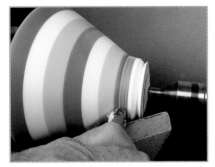

20 Reverse the bowl on the lathe using a small wooden cone to support the inside on the headstock and a small stebcentre on the tailstock. Square off the sides using the tungsten-tipped tool.

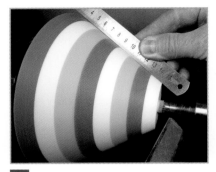

21 Check the sides for flatness and make any adjustments.

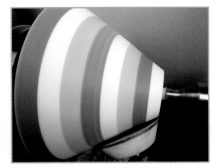

22 Sand the sides as for the inside.

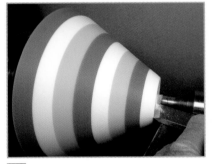

23 Hollow the base using a skew chisel on its side in shear-scraping mode.

24 Polish the bowl as before with the sheepskin buffer.

25 Now take it off the plate and remove the pip from the base using a carving chisel.

26 Once the base has been sanded the finished bowl should look like this.

POLYCHROMATIC OFFSET BOWL

Stunning effects can be obtained by mixing different-coloured
media – polychromatic. In this project we will make a pair of
offset bowls from plywood and Plexiglass (Perspex). The difficulty
has always been in finding glues that will effectively join plastics
to wood, but this has now been overcome and the choice
of media is no longer such a problem.

POLYCHROMATIC OFFSET BOWL

YOU WILL NEED:

EQUIPMENT
Circular saw
Bandsaw
Lathe
Disc sander

MATERIALS
1 sheet of 2³/₃₂in (18mm) good-quality birch plywood
Various sheets of Plexiglass acrylic
Flexible CA glue
Acrylic satin lacquer
9in (228mm) square x ½in (13mm) piece of MDF salvage

TOOLS
⅝in (16mm) bowl gouge
Tungsten-tipped shear scraper
Tungsten-tipped ring tool
Flat negative-rake scraper
Teardrop scraper
1in (50mm) parting tool

DESIGN

This design is based on the offset bowl developed for my popular Corian pieces, in which a cube is built up and then cut diagonally to create two offset bowls. Squares of 8in (203mm) plywood and Plexiglass are cut on the circular saw with a fine tungsten-tipped blade, then a cube of Plexiglass and plywood is built up. I put Plexiglass on the top and bottom, which would be the two circles on the inside and outside – plywood does not feather easily. I then placed several different coloured Plexiglass sheets together, rather than have an alternating pattern between plywood and Plexiglass.

Building up the composite

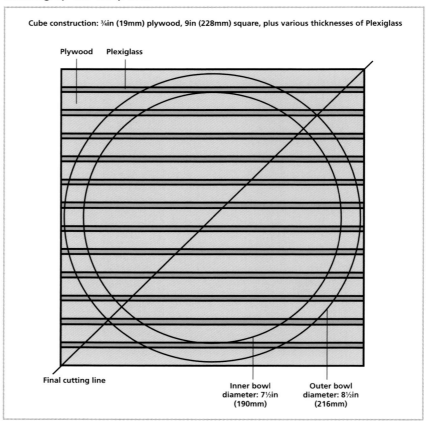

Cube construction: ¾in (19mm) plywood, 9in (228mm) square, plus various thicknesses of Plexiglass

Plywood   Plexiglass

Final cutting line

Inner bowl diameter: 7½in (190mm)

Outer bowl diameter: 8½in (216mm)

CUTTING AND CONSTRUCTION

1 Clamp the levels of plywood and Plexiglass together and draw a 6in (150mm) circle on one face to show the internal diameter of the bowls. This is used to determine the centre sections to be cut away before assembly. It is easier to cut away the waste now, before gluing up, than to try removing the waste later. The waste can be saved for future projects.

TIP: I had a few of the Plexiglass-to-wood joints fail in previous versions, but recalled a plasterer telling me that plaster has to have a key on which to stick. As a result I sandpapered the Plexiglass and cleaned off any greasy finger marks with methylated spirit for a perfect result.

2 Mount the centre sections individually in a large button-jaw chuck and cut out using a small parting tool. The large button-jaw chuck will take both square and round work.

SAFETY ADVICE: Be careful when cutting the plywood with the parting tool as it splinters. It is better to cut halfway through, and turn the square round and cut the other half from the back.

3 Stack up the levels to ensure that the cut-outs match the round internal shape. Sand and clean the Plexiglass with spirit, then glue the levels together using a medium-density flexible CA glue.

4 When the glue has cured (after about four hours), remove the cube from the jig and cut it diagonally on the bandsaw.

TIP: The Plexiglass sheet has a vinyl protective covering, which has to be removed before gluing.

SAFETY ADVICE: When using CA glues always wear disposable gloves and have adequate ventilation.

5 Remove as much of the waste material as you can before mounting the bowl on the lathe. Mark the rough shape of the bowl's outer rim with pencil. Taking slow cuts, cut off the corners on the bandsaw and, to avoid the machine overheating, do not push too hard.

6 Glue a wooden faceplate onto the base of the bowl to fit into the lathe.

7 Mount the composite on the lathe. Clean up the face of the composite, ready for a disc of 9in (330mm) wide MDF to be glued to it.

8 Glue the MDF disc on and support it with the tailstock. The MDF disc will hold the offset layers together while turning.

TURNING

9 Using either the bowl gouge in conventional bevel-rubbing mode or the tungsten-tipped shear scraper, remove the sharp corners from the sides and shape the base.

10 Gradually form the outside shape but do not turn down to the finished size as the strength of the extra wall thickness is needed to support the bowl while the inside is turned.

11 Cut the centre from the MDF faceplate with a parting tool and then with a tungsten-tipped shear scraper start to remove the sharp edges from the inside.

12 Use a teardrop scraper to refine the shape and eliminate tool marks.

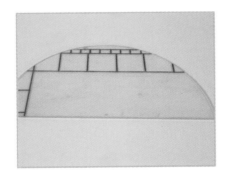

13 As the shape gets closer to the finished design, test it with a simple plastic template made to fit the inner radius.

14 With an offset design the inside has to be precisely cut otherwise inaccuracies will show up in the circular features of the bowl.

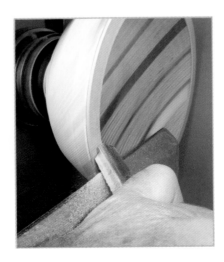

15 Now remove the bulk of the MDF disc, but leave a small, ⅛in (3mm) rim for support while turning the outside.

16 Now reverse the bowl on the lathe using an MDF cone on the headstock to support the rim while the outside is being brought down to its finished shape. (It is at this stage that I had two major disasters with previous versions as the joints failed and the bowl broke up into flying boomerangs around my workshop!) To eliminate the expansion strain on the bowl, I cut a ridge in the MDF cone to hold the re-glued bowl centrally without applying any lateral stress on it, and would recommend you do the same.

17 Centre the faceplate on the tailstock.

18 Rough the outside to almost finished shape with either the bowl gouge or the tungsten-tipped ring tool.

19 Use a negative-rake flat scraper to even out the ridges.

20 Now clean the top edge using the bowl gouge in upright shear-scraping mode.

21 Take the bowl off the lathe and check the wall thickness with your fingers, then re-mount it on its base and sand with Mirka Abronet discs, starting at 80 grit and working up to 400 grit. Be prepared to go back a few grits to eliminate scratches.

22 Part off the base from the faceplate, reverse the bowl and remount it on the MDF jam chuck. Centre the base with the tailstock using a small steb or ring centre that does not mark the base.

23 Now refine the shape of the bowl, cleaning up the sides with the flat negative-rake scraper.

24 Sand the outside with Mirka Abranet discs, starting at 80 and working up to 400 grit. Once removed from the lathe, take away the pip, sand and finish the base as required.

FINISHING

25 After sanding the bowl finish it with acrylic satin lacquer, applying three coats rubbed down in between coats with a fine abrasive pad or wire wool. Your finished bowl should look something like this.

OPEN-SEGMENT FLOWER VASE

This is an unusual design in that it looks like a fragile vertical stave construction but is actually made up of alternating open and closed segments of sycamore *(Acer pseudoplatanus)*. The closed segments are used to give the vase rigidity when turning and are removed later. The vase has been designed to take a tall glass vessel, so the base has been left open. The vase takes a total of about eight hours to make, but you will need to spread the work in stages over a week to allow for the adhesive and finish to dry.

OPEN-SEGMENT FLOWER VASE

YOU WILL NEED:

EQUIPMENT
Circular saw
Planer thicknesser
Mitre saw
Lathe and lathe steady
Drum sander
Bandsaw
Disc sander

MATERIALS
Ash *(Fraxinus spp.)*, box *(Buxus sempervirens)*, holly *(Ilex spp.)* or sycamore *(Acer pseudoplatanus)*
White PVA
Yellow aliphatic glue
Acrylic satin lacquer
8in (203mm) x ½in (13mm) piece of MDF salvage

TOOLS
⅝in (16mm) bowl gouge
Tungsten-tipped shear scraper
Flat negative-rake scraper
Teardrop scraper
Hollowing tool
Callipers
Warding file
Needle file

DESIGN

This is a 23 layer design with 11 open segment layers and 12 solid segment layers. The 18 segment SegEasy template uses a 4° angle, which gives a 20° segment with an 8° mitre angle. The base and the top level are 18-piece closed-segment rings with a 10° mitre angle. The open segment levels are all ¾in (19mm) thickness except the top level, which is ½in (13mm) thick. The separators are ⁵⁄₃₂in (4mm) thick and cut to a nine-segment design using a 20° mitre angle. The design was developed on Woodturner Studio, using its Bézier curve facility.

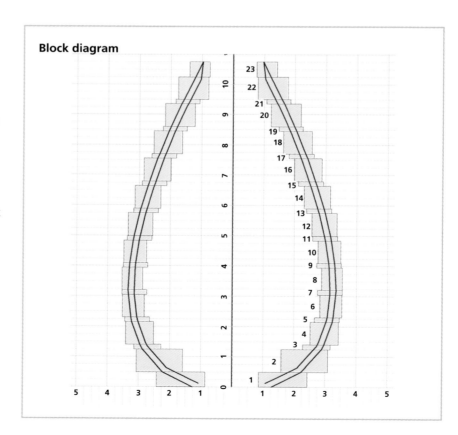

Block diagram

Cutting list

Layer no.	No. of segments		Outer radius	Inner radius	Length	Width	Mitre angle	Gap angle	Vessel radius	Board thickness	Board length	Edge radius
Base	18		2.426	0.867	0.856	1.560	10.000	0.000	2.226	0.500	14.586	2.464
2	18		3.075	1.583	0.864	1.492	8.000	4.000	2.875	0.750	15.829	3.105
3	9		3.156	2.265	2.297	0.891	20.000	0.000	2.956	0.150	20.210	3.358
4	18		3.421	2.504	0.961	0.917	8.000	4.000	3.221	0.750	18.954	3.454
5	9		3.453	2.639	2.514	0.814	20.000	0.000	3.253	0.150	22.382	3.675
6	18		3.538	2.821	0.994	0.717	8.000	4.000	3.338	0.750	20.024	3.572
7	9		3.542	2.759	2.578	0.782	20.000	0.000	3.342	0.150	23.054	3.769
8	18		3.542	2.881	0.996	0.661	8.000	4.000	3.342	0.750	20.178	3.577
9	9		3.510	2.719	2.555	0.792	20.000	0.000	3.310	0.150	22.822	3.736
10	18		3.496	2.753	0.983	0.743	8.000	4.000	3.296	0.750	19.749	3.530
11	9		3.383	2.585	2.463	0.798	20.000	0.000	3.183	0.150	21.970	3.600
12	18		3.357	2.549	0.943	0.808	8.000	4.000	3.157	0.750	18.890	3.390
13	9		3.181	2.379	2.316	0.802	20.000	0.000	2.981	0.150	20.634	3.385
14	18		3.141	2.285	0.883	0.855	8.000	4.000	2.941	0.750	17.684	3.172
15	9		2.918	2.122	2.124	0.796	20.000	0.000	2.718	0.150	18.926	3.105
16	18		2.870	1.973	0.807	0.896	8.000	4.000	2.670	0.750	16.214	2.898
17	9		2.607	1.817	1.898	0.790	20.000	0.000	2.407	0.150	16.907	2.774
18	18		2.549	1.615	0.717	0.934	8.000	4.000	2.349	0.750	14.503	2.574
19	9		2.248	1.471	1.636	0.777	20.000	0.000	2.048	0.150	14.594	2.392
20	18		2.185	1.217	0.614	0.968	8.000	4.000	1.985	0.750	12.578	2.206
21	9		1.850	1.087	1.347	0.763	20.000	0.000	1.650	0.150	12.027	1.969
22	18		1.779	0.787	0.500	0.992	8.000	4.000	1.579	0.750	10.467	1.796
Top	18		1.418	0.561	0.500	0.857	10.000	0.000	1.218	0.500	10.290	1.440

Measurements are in inches

Section view

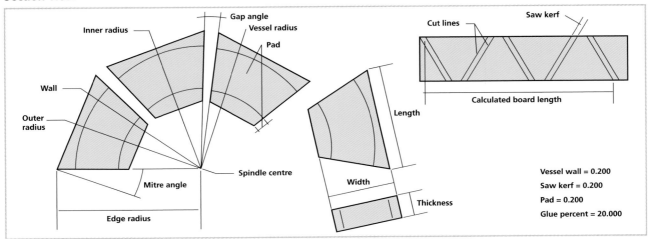

Vessel wall = 0.200
Saw kerf = 0.200
Pad = 0.200
Glue percent = 20.000

CUTTING AND CONSTRUCTION

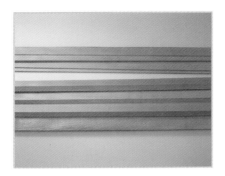

1 Cut the wood into the appropriate strips on the circular saw, before planing and thicknessing the thicker strips to a uniform thickness and sanding the thinner strips to thickness on the drum sander. Now size the strips to the appropriate width on the circular saw and plane the sawn face. It is important that the strips have a consistent thickness, as there is little room to handle discrepancies in the thickness of the segments during the build-up.

2 Cut the thinner ¼in (5mm) segments, used for the separators, on the bandsaw. Then cut all the ½in thick segments on the mitre saw.

3 Tidy up the ¼in (5mm) segments using the disc sander.

4 Glue together the thin segments with yellow aliphatic glue. Note that a nine-segment solid ring has to be glued up as one ring, so the angles must be accurate.

5 The top and bottom closed segment rings are made from 20° segments. Glue them up as semi-circles, square them up and then glue them up as rings. When the glue has cured, clean up the bottom face on the drum sander.

6 The vase is made from two bowl-type sections that are then turned inside before gluing together to form the vase. Mount the base ring and top ring onto wooden faceplates using glue paper joints.

7 Glue the base ring to the faceplate and centre it using an MDF backplate with concentric circles drawn on it.

8 Once the first solid level glue has cured, clean and face it ready for gluing the first open segment level.

9 Clean off any burr on the edges of the segments with a warding file and then assemble the segments on the template. Make sure that the grain direction is consistent. Glue up the first open-segment level and position it on the lathe between the base and the template, which is centred on the tailstock. Apply the glue with a fine artist's brush.

10 After positioning, adjust the tailstock to clamp the levels finger tight, and remove any excess glue with pipe cleaners. Leave eight hours between glue-ups.

11 The first closed-segment ring should now be glued to the open-segment ring. Position the join in the closed ring over a gap in the open-segment ring. This will mean that no intermediate joints will be seen after the separators are cut away. Repeat the process for the other levels, sanding flat each time and leaving eight hours between glue-ups. The lower vase section is from the base to level 7.

12 Build the top half of the vase as for the base. The top level is made using a closed-segment ring and glued to a new faceplate as before. This is level 23 (top) to level 8.

13 When the two halves have been constructed, the lower half will have a solid-segment ring for support...

14 ... but the top level will not.

15 Glue a disc of MDF to the top open segment level for support. The ring will act as a runway for the three-point lathe steady as well as support the open segments.

TURNING

16 Once the MDF support ring has been mounted in the bowl steady, clean up the inside with a hollowing tool.

17 When the inside has been roughed out, clean up with a tungsten-tipped shear scraper.

18 Achieve the final contour with a teardrop scraper.

19 It's easy to gauge wall thickness through the open segments. Aim for between ⅛–³⁄₁₆in (3–5mm) wall thickness. Make sure the contour is smooth – using your fingers to check is the best way.

20 Now mount the base section on the lathe. Since it is only seven levels and has a solid top ring, it will not need the support of the bowl steady. Make a hole in the base and the top for the glass vase using a 55mm saw-tooth Forstner bit.

21 Us the same technique for turning the base as for the top.

22 Now comes the difficult bit. To ensure both halves will fit together seamlessly, the internal diameters have to be exactly the same as well as the contour leading up to that join. The join has been picked at the widest section – the point where both inside edges are vertical. It takes a bit of trial and error using callipers to get the shape and dimensions correct.

23 When both parts fit together, sand the insides as you will not be able to access them after joining.

24 Cut away the MDF ring on the top half with the bowl gouge and square off the open-segment layer with the sanding disc. Glue both parts together with white PVA glue and hold in the lathe to stand for eight hours.

25 The finished composite vase should look something like this.

26 Before turning the outside of the composite, remove the wooden faceplate at the top by breaking the glue joint with a sharp knife and a hammer.

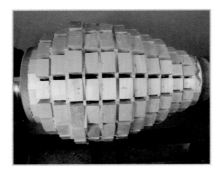

27 Position the composite on the lathe with the base faceplate in the chuck and the top supported by a tapered jam chuck on the tailstock.

28 Establish the final shape using the bowl gouge in shear-scraping mode working from the tailstock end (the top of the vase) to the headstock end (the base of the vase).

29 Make the final finish using a flat negative-rake scraper, slowly drawn along the contour.

30 The partly finished vase should now should look something like this.

31 The best way to cut away the thin supporting separators is by using a small gent's dovetail saw, but take care not to catch the saw in the vertical spines, as these can no longer be turned after the stringer supports have been cut away. Start at the top – tailstock end – and gradually work down the vessel, level by level, to maintain the strength of the composite while cutting.

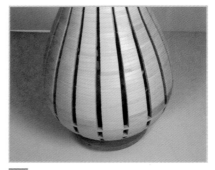

32 The stringers are gradually removed starting at the top and working to the base.

FINISHING

33 Once all the stringers have been removed, the sawn edges can be filed and sanded away. Use a small needle file to remove the sharp edges.

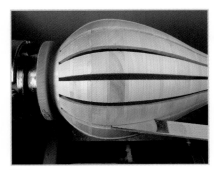

34 A small sanding disc attached to Velcro that has been glued to a thin strip of wood works very well in sanding the inside of the staves flat.

35 To finish off the base of the vase, it has to be removed from its faceplate. A glue joint is easily separated using a sharp knife and a gentle tap from a hammer.

36 To finish off the underside, remount the vase on a jam chuck on the headstock, but with the base at the tailstock end. Clean up the base. Once the shape has been established you can sand the outside, starting at 120 grit and working up to 400 grit.

37 Acrylic lacquer spray works well but beware runs. Apply three coats of clear acrylic satin lacquer. After each coat is dry, burnish the vase with either wire-wool or an abrasive pad to remove any raised fibres and dust. This finished piece should look like this.

Open-segment Candlesticks

Creating sleek open-segment objects is a challenge; in this project we create a template to enable these candlesticks to be easily built. For such elegant candlesticks I chose cherry (*Prunus avium*) and sycamore (*Acer pseudoplatanus*) planked and dried but any strong, white hardwoods can be used. The wood has to be very dry to prevent the segments from cracking. Mixing two different types of wood is not a problem because the candlesticks will be sprayed with black ebonizing lacquer later. The pair takes about 10 hours to make, but in stages spread over two weeks to allow for the adhesive and finish to dry.

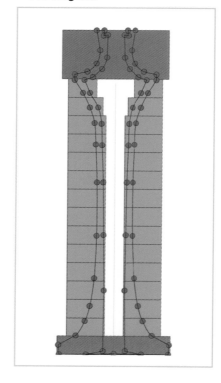

OPEN-SEGMENT CANDLESTICKS

Skill level:
● **Advanced**

YOU WILL NEED:

EQUIPMENT
Circular saw
Planer thicknesser
Mitre saw
Lathe and lathe steady
Rotary bowl sander
Bandsaw (optional)

MATERIALS
Sycamore *(Acer pseudoplatanus)* and cherry *(Prunus avium)*
White PVA
Black ebonizing lacquer
Acrylic satin lacquer
Candle cups

TOOLS
⅝in (16mm) bowl gouge
Tungsten-tipped shear scraper
Long negative-rake side scraper
Hollowing tool
Parting tool
Needle file

TEMPLATE
Base – 12in (305mm) square piece of ¾in (19mm) MDF
Segments – 12in (305mm) square piece of ½in (13mm) MDF
Separators – 1 piece 40in x ⅛in x 1in (1m x 3mm x 25mm)

DESIGN

Since the SegEasy plates featured in the earlier projects are only available in 18 and 24 segments per layer, which would not allow such a narrow waist, a template must be created. The composite has 16 layers with eight segments per layer and ⅛in (3mm) fixed-width separation, plus a solid layer on the bottom and the top. The intermediate levels are all ½in (13mm) thickness.

The fixed width template is easy to construct and gives a very pleasing design. A fixed-width separator between the segments does not change the segment angle, so for an eight-segment design the segment angle is 22.5° degrees.

The candlestick design was developed using a more advanced computer programme called Woodturner Pro, which can handle the various complex angles as well as the constant-thickness separators.

The composite side walls have been designed to be quite thick, initially to support the hollowing as construction progresses. They are then reduced to the finished dimensions after construction when the candlestick can be supported and turned between centres.

Block diagram

Cutting list

Row	Type	Segments		Board thickness	Diameter outside	Diameter inside	Segment edge length	Vertical spacer width	Board width	Economy board length	Mitre angle
16	Disk cherry	8	■	2	3	0.5	1.11	0.13	1.27	29.18	22.5°
15	Flat sycamore	8	▦	0.5	3	0.5	1.11	0.13	1.27	29.18	22.5°
14	Flat sycamore	8	▦	0.5	3	0.5	1.11	0.13	1.27	29.18	22.5°
13	Flat sycamore	8	▦	0.5	3	0.5	1.11	0.13	1.27	29.18	22.5°
12	Flat sycamore	8	▦	0.5	3	0.5	1.11	0.13	1.27	29.18	22.5°
11	Flat sycamore	8	▦	0.5	3	0.5	1.11	0.13	1.27	29.18	22.5°
10	Flat sycamore	8	▦	0.5	3	0.5	1.11	0.13	1.27	29.18	22.5°
9	Flat sycamore	8	▦	0.5	3	0.5	1.11	0.13	1.27	29.18	22.5°
8	Flat sycamore	8	▦	0.5	3	0.5	1.11	0.13	1.27	29.18	22.5°
7	Flat sycamore	8	▦	0.5	3	0.5	1.11	0.13	1.27	29.18	22.5°
6	Flat sycamore	8	▦	0.5	3	0.5	1.11	0.13	1.27	29.18	22.5°
5	Flat sycamore	8	▦	0.5	3	0.5	1.11	0.13	1.27	29.18	22.5°
4	Flat sycamore	8	▦	0.5	3	0.5	1.11	0.13	1.27	29.18	22.5°
3	Flat sycamore	8	▦	0.5	3	0.5	1.11	0.13	1.27	29.18	22.5°
2	Flat sycamore	8	▦	0.5	3	0.5	1.11	0.13	1.27	29.18	22.5°
1	Disk cherry	8	■	0.5	3.5						

Measurements are in inches

Template layout

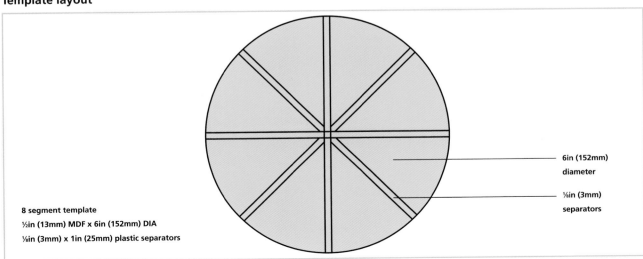

8 segment template
½in (13mm) MDF x 6in (152mm) DIA
⅛in (3mm) x 1in (25mm) plastic separators

6in (152mm) diameter

⅛in (3mm) separators

CUTTING AND CONSTRUCTION

1 The construction of the template is just like building a closed-segment layer. A strip of ⅛ x 1in (3 x 25mm) plastic strip – available from DIY stores – will be used as the separator. I find it easier to mark out the baseplate first, prior to gluing up.

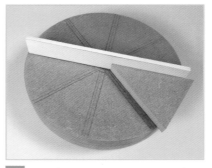

2 Cut the segments at 22.5° using ½in (13mm) MDF. Mount them on a ¾in (19mm) thick piece of either MDF or plywood 12in (30cm) square.

3 Glue the segments and separators in place, one at a time.

4 Clean up the template edges to a 6⅝in (170mm) circular disc on the bandsaw.

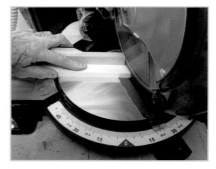

SAFETY ADVICE: When using the mitre saw, remember to keep your fingers clear of the blade.

5 Cut the segments on a mitre saw. The dimensions should be within plus or minus ¹⁄₁₆in (1.5mm). The mitre saw should be set to 22.5° for these segments. A very clean cut can be obtained by slowly lowering the spinning blade onto the wood.

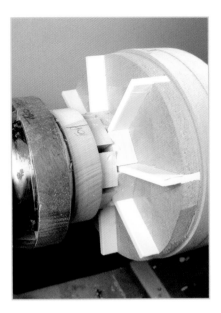

6 The base of the candlestick is solid. Start by gluing the base onto a wooden faceplate already set up to fit the chuck jaws; this saves wood in the base and gives more room to part off the finished piece. Before gluing, ensure that both faces are flat.

7 When the glue has cured, clean up the base and sand it level for the first row of segments. Glue both surfaces – the segments on the template and the level on the lathe – using a glue brush. Glue up the first level using white PVA and position it on the lathe between the base and the template, which is centred on the tailstock. After positioning, adjust the tailstock to clamp the levels finger tight.

8 Remove any excess glue with wet pipe cleaners. Once the glue has dried, the next level can be constructed. To ensure the segments are all the same height, sand the glued-up level on the lathe at a very slow speed, with hardly any pressure from the tailstock, and using 120-grit sandpaper wedged between the level and a large MDF backplate. If your lathe does not have speed control then manually turn the composite structure against the sandpaper. Scribble pencil lines on each segment before sanding and keep up the action until all the pencil lines are gone.

9 Line up the segment levels brickwork fashion. With open-segment work the truing-up of the alignment is made very easy by looking through the structure and seeing the corresponding open segments on the other side, the gaps showing up any misalignment.

10 In order to have the centre hollow, after every three rows drill out the centre using a 1in (25mm) saw-tooth Forstner bit held in a drill chuck in the tailstock. Set the lathe speed at about 1,000rpm, to avoid the drill tearing the first segments. Very slowly approach the first segments until the drill has centred itself and started to cut a side wall. Keep clearing the cuttings away to avoid them clogging up and breaking the fragile structure. Drill through the base level as well so that the inside can be accessed later from the bottom. This process should be repeated every three levels, each set of cuts meeting up with the previous set.

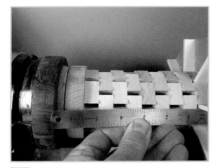

11 Gradually build up the levels, letting each one dry for eight hours before sanding it flat and gluing the next level. Alignment is very important as you reach the top levels. Continue to clean any excess glue from the gaps.

12 Continue to build up the stem.

13 As the top levels are approached the inner radius becomes larger and a bigger drill can be used to clean them up prior to hollowing.

14 Create the flare inside the top levels by using a tungsten-tipped shear scraper. Again, set the lathe speed relatively high at 1000rpm and take very light cuts. The structure has no support at this stage, so remove slithers of wood very slowly until you achieve the finished profile.

15 Clean up the inside using sandpaper held in a ½in (13mm) steel tube that has been cut at one end to hold a small 120-grit sanding disc. Move the tube up and down the inside with the lathe speed set very slow, 50 rpm, or if that is not available turn the candlestick by hand. You can progress through the grits but the inside will not be accessible, so 180 grit is as far as you're likely to go.

16 Before the solid top segment is glued into place it is advisable to spray the black ebonizing lacquer inside the candlestick. Take care to avoid runs and clogging the gaps between the segments – a couple of light passes is all that is required. The top solid segment can now be glued in place. Make sure that the open-segment level is perfectly flat beforehand, using the sanding disc on the tailstock. Clear any excess glue using wet pipe cleaners.

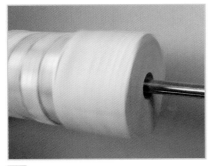

17 Now drill out the top of the candlestick to take the candle cups.

18 These solid brass cups have a flange so the outer radius must first be cut to the required depth of the flange using a parting tool before the inner diameter is turned to fit the cup. I have found that these holders are all slightly different shapes so it is best to fit them individually.

TURNING

19 Woodturners have a habit of sticking their fingers inside hollow forms to feel what the finish is like, so it is best to undercut the base of the top section to follow the external curve. Hollow the inside using a long side scraper. Take care not to touch the painted interior.

20 Using a small round jam centre that fixes over the revolving centre to enable the candlestick to be centred and supported on the tailstock, shape the solid top segment to a rough candle-holder shape – you need all the strength of the composite structure to get this right before reducing the wall thickness of the sides. You could use a spindle gouge for this shaping but I prefer my bowl gouge.

21 The outside of the open segments can now be cleaned up using the bowl gouge in its conventional bevel-rubbing mode. The glued segments do burn the edge so the gouge has to be constantly resharpened.

22 When the stem is running true, the easiest way to turn the outside wall is by using the bowl gouge on its side in shear-scraping mode. A shear scraper can be used but the finish from the bowl gouge is much better. Reduce the size in stages to give maximum thickness always towards the driven end (base) of the candlestick, otherwise it can snag and break up very quickly.

23 Start turning at the top third of the candlestick.

24 Gradually move down the candlestick, turning one third at a time, taking each section to a finished thickness.

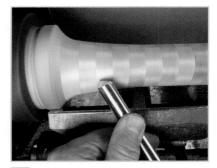

25 Once one candlestick has been roughed down, stop there and repeat the process for the other one. It is not too late at this stage to make sizing adjustments.

FINISHING

26 When both candlesticks have identical height and cross-section dimensions they can be sanded down using a rotary bowl sander. Start at 120 grit and work up to 400 grit. Finish off the top and the base by hand. Clean any burrs in the gaps with a needle file.

27 While the candlesticks are still mounted on their bases, it is wise to apply the first coat of ebonizing lacquer. Once dry they can be remounted in the lathe and sanded again. Part off the candlestick and remount between jam chucks.

28 Clean up and hollow the base. Remove from the lathe and sand as necessary.

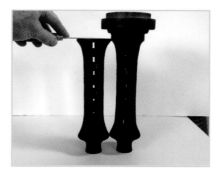

29 Marry up the two candlesticks – but upside down – and mark equal heights on the other candlestick. This one can then be parted off to that line and the two should be of identical height.

30 Fine sand using an abrasive pad on the inside and outside prior to spraying. Ebonizing acrylic lacquer spray works well but take care to avoid runs. Apply three coats after each one is dry, burnishing the candlestick with either wire wool or an abrasive pad to remove any raised fibres and dust. Finish with two coats of gloss acrylic lacquer so that they look like this.

GHERKIN LAMP STAND

The design for this lamp stand was developed many years ago, but it has become so popular that I keep returning to it. It is named after the Gherkin Tower building in the City of London, which has a similar spiral. The lamp takes about 15 hours to make, in stages spread over three weeks to allow for the adhesive to cure.

GHERKIN LAMP STAND

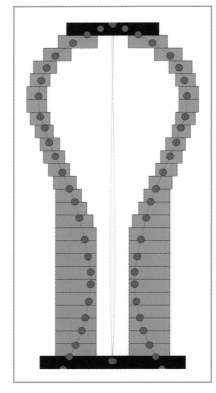

YOU WILL NEED:

EQUIPMENT
Circular saw
Planer thicknesser
Bandsaw
Lathe and lathe steady
SegEasy template, 24 segment

MATERIALS
Sycamore *(Acer pseudoplatanus)*
Mahogany *(Meliaceae)*
Clear PVA
Yellow aliphatic glue
Acrylic satin lacquer

TOOLS
¾in (19mm) bowl gouge
Tungsten-tipped shear scraper
Long negative-rake side scraper
Teardrop scraper
Hollowing tool
Callipers
Skew chisel
Needle file

DESIGN

The basic design comprises a 24-piece segment ring with four coloured segments used to create the spiral. My early version was made from ebony *(Diospyros spp.)* and boxwood *(Buxus sempervirens)* but it split after a few weeks. The wood was not very dry and when the finished piece was moved around different places, with different humidities, it expanded and contracted but not evenly; the ebony spiral broke away from the boxwood. The effects of the expansion are of course aggravated by the design, as all of the ebony pieces are connected together, therefore multiplying the effects of the expansion.

Sycamore and mahogany seem to be a lot more tolerant of each other; certainly the mahogany is a lot easier to turn than the ebony. This time I used sycamore that had been drying for more than ten years and mahogany from some library bookcase shelves that were over 100 years old.

The lamp composite is constructed in two halves to allow the inside shape to be established – it is not accessible afterwards. The SegEasy 24-segment template is mounted on two layers of ¾in (19mm) MDF to give it support. The design was created in 3D Design PRO and then built in Woodturner PRO. It has 27 levels, all ½in (13mm) thick.

Block diagram

Cutting list

Row	Type	Segments	Board thickness	Diameter outside	Diameter inside	Segment edge length	Vertical spacer width	Board width	Economy board length	Mitre angle
27	Mahogany	■	0.5	3.5						
26	Sycamore and Mahogany	20 4 ■	0.5	4.13	1.18	0.4	0.14	1.48	78.33	5.55°
25	Sycamore and Mahogany	20 4 ■	0.5	5.25	3.15	0.51	0.18	1.06	81.88	5.55°
24	Sycamore and Mahogany	20 4 ■	0.5	6	4.25	0.58	0.2	0.88	84.01	5.55°
23	Sycamore and Mahogany	20 4 ■	0.5	6.25	4.75	0.61	0.21	0.76	84.87	5.55°
22	Sycamore and Mahogany	20 4 ■	0.5	6.5	5	0.63	0.22	0.76	85.46	5.55°
21	Sycamore and Mahogany	20 4 ■	0.5	6.5	5	0.63	0.22	0.76	85.46	5.55°
20	Sycamore and Mahogany	20 4 ■	0.5	6.25	4.75	0.61	0.21	0.76	84.87	5.55°
19	Sycamore and Mahogany	20 4 ■	0.5	5.88	4.5	0.57	0.2	0.7	84.14	5.55°
18	Sycamore and Mahogany	20 4 ■	0.5	5.5	4	0.53	0.19	0.76	83.13	5.55°
17	Sycamore and Mahogany	20 4 ■	0.5	5.25	3.63	0.51	0.18	0.82	82.41	5.55°
16	Sycamore and Mahogany	20 4 ■	0.5	4.88	3.25	0.47	0.17	0.82	81.54	5.55°
15	Sycamore and Mahogany	20 4 ■	0.5	4.5	2.75	0.44	0.15	0.88	80.52	5.55°
14	Sycamore and Mahogany	20 4 ■	0.5	4.33	2.36	0.42	0.15	0.99	79.89	5.55°
13	Sycamore and Mahogany	20 4 ■	0.5	4.33	1.97	0.42	0.15	1.19	79.45	5.55°
12	Sycamore and Mahogany	20 4 ■	0.5	4.33	1.5	0.42	0.15	1.42	78.93	5.55°
11	Sycamore and Mahogany	20 4 ■	0.5	4.33	1.25	0.42	0.15	1.54	78.65	5.55°
10	Sycamore and Mahogany	20 4 ■	0.5	4.33	1.25	0.42	0.15	1.54	78.65	5.55°
9	Sycamore and Mahogany	20 4 ■	0.5	4.33	1.25	0.42	0.15	1.54	78.65	5.55°
8	Sycamore and Mahogany	20 4 ■	0.5	4.33	1.25	0.42	0.15	1.54	78.65	5.55°
7	Sycamore and Mahogany	20 4 ■	0.5	4.33	1.25	0.42	0.15	1.54	78.65	5.55°
6	Sycamore and Mahogany	20 4 ■	0.5	4.33	1.25	0.42	0.15	1.54	78.65	5.55°
5	Sycamore and Mahogany	20 4 ■	0.5	4.33	1.25	0.42	0.15	1.54	78.65	5.55°
4	Sycamore and Mahogany	20 4 ■	0.5	4.33	1.25	0.42	0.15	1.54	78.65	5.55°
3	Sycamore and Mahogany	20 4 ■	0.5	4.33	1.25	0.42	0.15	1.54	78.65	5.55°
2	Sycamore and Mahogany	20 4 ■	0.5	4.33	1.25	0.42	0.15	1.54	78.65	5.55°
1	Mahogany	■	0.5	5.51						

Measurements are in inches

CUTTING AND CONSTRUCTION

1 Cut the base and top to size on the bandsaw, then glue them to the wooden faceplate to fit the chuck.

2 A paper-glue joint will enable the maximum thickness of the mahogany to be retained and allow it to be easily parted from the faceplate. Apply either PVA or aliphatic resin glue to both sides of the glossy paper.

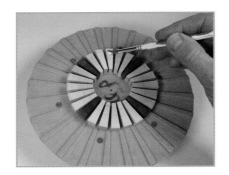

3 Position the segments for the first level on the SegEasy template. Ensure the grain direction is uniform and the four mahogany segments are equally spaced. A quick-drying PVA glue that dries clear is preferred for work with light-coloured woods; the aliphatic yellow glue leaves a dark yellow line. Brush glue onto the segments and the base. By using the glue sparingly on both surfaces it will make cleaning up of excess glue easier.

4 Centre the SegEasy template on the tailstock and slowly bring it up to the base. A rubber band wrapped around the segments prevents them falling out. Gradually apply pressure from the tailstock and ensure all the segments are pushed firmly down into the template. Remove excess glue with damp pipe cleaners.

5 The next layer can now be assembled, but first check the position of the next mahogany segment with the template and the composite. It's best to mark the top of the SegEasy template and the base of the composite to ensure they are always aligned, as there will be slight discrepancies. Sand the glued level flat before gluing the next level.

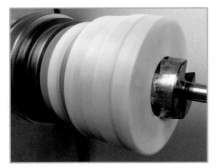

6 At the 5th level, drill out the base column using a Forstner-type, 2in (50mm) self-centring drill. Repeat the drilling process at appropriate intervals.

7 Gradually glue and assemble the levels.

8 At level 12, glue an MDF disc to the segments to act as a support in the lathe steady.

TURNING

9 The MDF ring is then trued up ready for the three-point steady and the centre of the MDF disc drilled out ready for turning.

10 Mount the composite in the lathe steady and tidy up the inside, remove the drill marks and start the flare, using a tungsten-tipped shear scraper to establish the finished size.

11 Smooth the inside using a long negative-rake side scraper.

12 Cut away the MDF support ring and sand the open segments flat. Start building up the remaining open segment levels to level 21.

13 After gluing an MDF support disc to level 21, start turning the composite. With a 600rpm lathe speed, first remove the rough edges with the hollowing tool until the composite is revolving evenly.

14 Bring the sides to approximately the finished shape using the tungsten-tipped shear scraper.

15 Now establish and smooth the inside contour with the teardrop scraper. The inside shape will govern the outside shape so particular attention has to be given to this stage. It's important to remember that the two halves will be joined together where the top inner segments' contour is almost at right angles to the top level, not at an angle; otherwise the inside will have a valley shape rather than a circular one.

16 After bringing the wall width down to about ³⁄₁₆in (5mm) or more, depending on your preference (and confidence), sand the inside, starting at 120 grit and working up to 400 grit. Finally, remove the top MDF ring and sand the top level ready for gluing to the top section.

17 The top composite section is constructed in the same way, an MDF disc being glued to the 22nd level to support the composite while turning the inside. It is easier to drill a hole in the top at this stage to accommodate the light fitting; it will provide a centre later for turning. Hollow out the top composite as for the base, using callipers to ensure that the rim's inside diameter is the same size as the base's.

18 When the inside of the composite has been turned and sanded, remove the MDF ring with a bowl gouge in almost vertical shear-scraping mode, clean up the open segments and sand them level ready for gluing to the bottom half.

19 Carefully brush glue onto the tops of both halves and glue them together. Hold the base in the headstock and the top in the tailstock, applying moderate pressure. Remove any excess glue with damp pipe cleaners. Leave the composite a day to completely dry out before turning.

20 It is best to remove the wooden faceplate from the top of the composite before turning. Centre the top on the tailstock using the previously drilled hole supported by a conical tailstock.

21 Starting at the top of the composite, carefully remove the rough corners using a bowl gouge in conventional bevel-rubbing mode. Once the edges of the composite have been removed and it is revolving evenly, use the bowl gouge in shear-scraping mode, first on its side and later in almost vertical mode to take very fine shavings when the bowl thickness gets down to finished size. Gradually work down the bowl in stages. (It is difficult to go back to the top once the thickness has been reduced because it will start to vibrate.)

22 When the shape is finished, sand the outside, starting at 120 grit and working up to 400 grit. Remove any burrs and whiskers using a needle file.

FINISHING

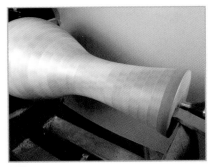

23 Before it is removed from its faceplate, apply a couple of coats of lacquer to enable it to be sanded on the lathe between each coat. I do not use sanding sealer on mixed wood composites as the colour may run. Split the base from the faceplate as before and reverse the composite on the lathe to finish off the base. The hole in the top allows it to be mounted on the headstock using a spigot, the base being supported on the tailstock using a small stebcentre. Make sure the composite base is revolving centrally and then clean up the underside using a bowl gouge in shear-scraping mode and finally tidying up with a skew chisel in negative-rake mode.

24 Now apply several coats of silk-finish lacquer, cleaning the surface with an abrasive pad between coats, and then clean up the gaps in the segments with a needle file. The finished lamp stand should look something like this.

SKELETON CANDLESTICKS

For these elegant candlesticks I have used ebony *(Diospyros spp.)*
and holly *(Ilex spp.)*, the two extremes in the colour spectrum. The
ebony is a challenge, as it is a very hard wood to turn. The holly,
on the other hand, is beautiful to turn but a lot softer than ebony.
The holly will become contaminated with the ebony sanding dust
but that can be alleviated. I made earlier versions of the design
with ash *(Fraxinus spp.)* and sycamore *(Acer pseudoplatanus)*,
which also work well with ebony. These candlesticks take about
ten hours to make, in stages spread over ten days to allow for
the adhesive to cure.

SKELETON CANDLESTICKS

YOU WILL NEED:

EQUIPMENT

Circular saw
Planer thicknesser
Planer jointer
Mitre saw
Lathe and lathe steady
Bandsaw
Disc sander

MATERIALS

Holly *(Ilex spp.)*
Ebony *(Diospyros spp.)*
White PVA
Yellow aliphatic glue
Acrylic satin lacquer
Brass cups
6in (152mm) x ½in (13mm) piece
of MDF salvage

TOOLS

¾in (19mm) bowl gouge
Tungsten-tipped shear scraper
Long negative-rake side scraper
Half-round negative-rake scraper
Kidney-shaped hand scraper
Parting tool
Needle file

DESIGN

With this design I wanted to produce an elegant open-segment piece that looked like a stave construction. I have constructed one version with the separators made from the same wood as the uprights, to lessen the impact of the separators, but it was not as pleasing on the eye as the black ebony version.

The design uses a variable-width eight-segment template, which I had to manufacture myself as no commercial template was available. Alternatively, the composite can be constructed by gluing each segment separately using Bill Smith's jig, discussed on page 66.

Block diagram

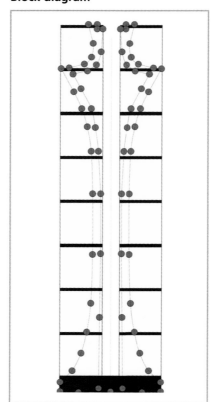

The complex design was developed in 3D Design Pro and exported to Woodturner Pro to build up the segments. The segment design for the stem has been purposely taken oversize to support the delicate composite when turning the top.

Cutting list

Row	Type	Segments		Board thickness	Diameter outside	Diameter inside	Segment edge length	Vertical spacer width	Board width	Economy board length	Mitre angle
17	Flat ebony	8	■	0.08	3	0.5	1.24	0	1.27	30.26	22.5°
16	Open-segment holly	8	□	1.25	3	0.5	0.91	0.3	1.26	28.6	16.88°
15	Flat ebony	8	■	0.08	3	0.5	1.24	0	1.27	30.26	22.5°
14	Open-segment holly	8	□	1.25	3	0.5	0.91	0.3	1.26	28.6	16.88°
13	Flat ebony	8	■	0.09	3	0.5	1.24	0	1.27	30.26	22.5°
12	Open-segment holly	8	□	1.25	3	0.5	0.91	0.3	1.26	28.6	16.88°
11	Flat ebony	8	■	0.08	3	0.5	1.24	0	1.27	30.26	22.5°
10	Open-segment holly	8	□	1.25	3	0.5	0.91	0.3	1.26	28.6	16.88°
9	Flat ebony	8	■	0.08	3	0.5	1.24	0	1.27	30.26	22.5°
8	Open-segment holly	8	□	1.25	3	0.5	0.91	0.3	1.26	28.6	16.88°
7	Flat ebony	8	■	0.09	3	0.5	1.24	0	1.27	30.26	22.5°
6	Open-segment holly	8	□	1.25	3	0.5	0.91	0.3	1.26	28.6	16.88°
5	Flat ebony	8	■	0.08	3	0.5	1.24	0	1.27	30.26	22.5°
4	Open-segment holly	8	□	1.25	3	0.5	0.91	0.3	1.26	28.6	16.88°
3	Flat ebony	8	■	0.08	3	0.5	1.24	0	1.27	30.26	22.5°
2	Open-segment holly	8	□	1.25	3	0.5	0.91	0.3	1.26	28.6	16.88°
1	Disk ebony	8	■	0.5	3						

Measurements are in inches

CUTTING AND CONSTRUCTION

1 After cutting the wood to size, planing and thicknessing it, cut the holly segments on the mitre saw set to a 17° mitre angle.

2 Plane one side of the ebony strip and then cut it slightly oversize on the bandsaw. The strips should be about ⅛in (3mm) thick at this stage; the thickness will be reduced on the lathe later to about ¹⁄₁₆in (1.5mm). The circular saw could be used but the wider blade wastes so much of this valuable material. They are left un-planed on the other side as this will be sanded later.

3 Cut the ebony segments on the bandsaw at a mitre angle of 22.5°.

4 Clean up on the disc sander.

5 Glue the ebony rings into half circles with the planed side down.

6 True them up on the disc sander.

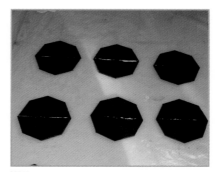

7 Glue them into full rings. As you are gluing end-grain, make sure you use yellow aliphatic glue.

8 Allow about four hours for the glue to attain full strength on these thin rings, then clean it off the flat side by gently pushing the rings against the disc sander.

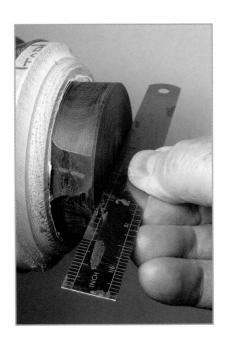

9 After cleaning up the corners of the ebony base on the bandsaw, attach the base to the wooden faceplate using a paper-glue joint. True up the base with a bowl gouge and sand the base flat.

10 Pay particular attention to grain direction when positioning the first row of holly segments on the template. With no end-grain to glue, a white quick-drying PVA glue is suitable for this level. Apply it to all the segments and the ebony base with a small artist's paint brush.

11 Using the tailstock to support the segment template, position it on the ebony base, apply pressure and remove any excess glue. Allow to dry, then clean up the first level of segments with the bowl gouge in almost vertical shear-scraping mode, and then with the sanding disc. Now glue the ebony ring to the first level, applying white PVA to both the holly and the ebony with a fine brush. The ring is positioned by the tailstock with an MDF backplate and a piece of foam to take up any irregularities and to provide a constant pressure over the whole of the disc.

TURNING

12 When dry, clean up with the bowl gouge in shear-scraping mode, reducing the ebony disc to about ¹⁄₁₆in (1.5mm) and sanding flat. Repeat the process for the next level, as shown.

13 At the 5th level, drill the centre of the composite using a ½in (13mm) Forstner drill bit mounted on the tailstock. Cut the hole right through the base so that access to the inside can be made after the composite has been glued up.

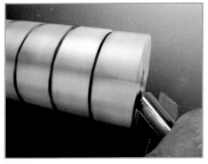

14 Glue and true the remaining levels.

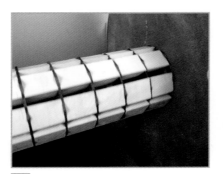

15 Drill the centre every four levels until the top level of the body, level 15, is reached, then true up and sand the top, ebony, level.

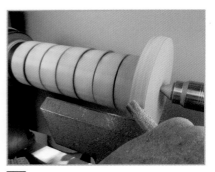

16 Glue, centre and true up an MDF disc to the top level to act as the support for the composite in the lathe steady.

17 Drill the top using a 1½in (38mm) Forstner drill to open up the flare, taking care not to drill too deeply.

18 Open up the flare using the tungsten-tipped shear scraper or any conventional small half-round scraper in shear-scraper mode.

19 To ensure that both candlesticks are near identical I usually make a template from thin Plexiglass to follow the contour of the inside.

20 Tidy up the inside using the long negative-rake side scraper.

21 Then sand using a sanding disc mounted on a split metal tube.

22 Now cut away the MDF disc with the bowl gouge and sand the top flat, ready to take the candleholder, so that the finished inside looks something like this.

23 Now the candleholder is constructed by mounting the holly segments on the template and gluing them to a wooden faceplate using a paper glue joint.

24 Cut the ebony segments on the mitre saw. For my jig they are 5.5°.

25 When the glued-up holly top section has cured, glue up the ebony segments between the holly segments using yellow aliphatic glue. Do not apply too much pressure or the holly segments will become detached from the faceplate, but do make sure that they fit snugly.

26 When the glue has cured, mount the faceplates in the lathe and clean up the inside of the candleholder.

27 Drill the centre to accept the brass cups. The brass cups that I use vary in size so I check the dimension of the cup to be used before drilling.

28 Flare the inside towards the sides that will be glued, being careful not to make the flare too deep or intrude on the flat area to be glued to the base. Check the dimensions against the composite to make sure they will marry up correctly.

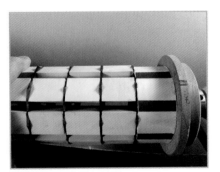

29 Glue the candleholder to the composite using white PVA, then centre the wooden faceplate on the tailstock and apply pressure. Make sure the ebony segments line up with the gaps on the lower section.

30 After about four hours, remove the top wooden faceplate from the composite…

31 … by cutting it away with a tap of a hammer on a sharp knife.

32 Mount the base of the composite candlestick on the lathe and true up the top to accept the top ebony ring.

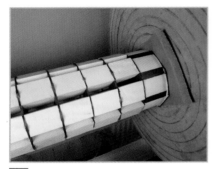

33 Glue the ebony ring to the top and position it using a small square of foam sandwiched in the wooden backplate.

34 After about four hours centre the top on the tailstock and turn this section into a round barrel shape to act as a runway on the lathe steady for cutting the opening for the brass candle cup.

35 True up the top ebony ring, turn it down to about ³⁄₃₂in (2.5mm) to allow for the brass cup, then drill out the cup hole to size.

36 Cut out the rebate for the brass cup using a parting tool and a side scraper.

37 Trim the top to accept the cup.

38 After removing the lathe steady and supporting the composite again on the tailstock using a wooden jam chuck, turn the candleholder top using a bowl or spindle gouge.

39 Clean up with a half-round negative-rake scraper.

40 Bring the sides gradually down to finished size, starting with the top two sections, cutting these back initially with the bowl gouge in bevel rubbing mode.

41 As the wall starts to get thinner, use the bowl gouge in shear-scraping mode to bring down to size plus an extra ¹⁄₁₆in (1.5mm) thickness at this stage for final cleaning up later.

42 Now bring the next two sections down to size and then the last two sections. Initially, the bowl gouge should be used in conventional bevel-rubbing mode to remove the excess wood.

TIP: Keep the gouge very sharp and almost vertical to ensure it does not snag the delicate shape. Sometimes at this stage a segment can start to get unstuck – the sound of the tool will change. Stop the lathe before it becomes serious and just use a small amount of thin CA glue to penetrate the joint. Leave for 20 minutes and it will be fine.

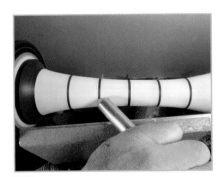

43 Take the bottom section down to size and establish the curve to the base. With the shape established, carefully smooth it out using long sweeping strokes of the bowl gouge in shear-scraping mode.

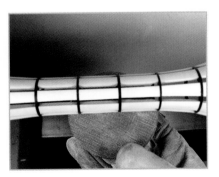

44 When the shape has been turned to your satisfaction (I usually aim for a wall thickness of ⅛in/3mm but you may want to play safe) the outside can be sanded with a flat sanding disc. Start at 200 and work up to 320 grit initially.

45 Remove ebony dust from the holly fibres of the candleholder by using a kidney-shaped hand scraper with the lathe turning very slowly. Do not sand this area again!

46 Part the candlestick from the wooden faceplate.

47 Reverse and mount the candlestick on the lathe using jam chucks to hold the two ends. Using a spindle gouge in shear-scraping mode, clean up the base and hollow the centre so that it does not wobble.

48 After sanding the base, remove the candlestick from the chuck to allow for the inside to be sanded again but this time from the base using wooden dowelling cut to accept a sanding disc.

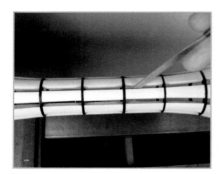

49 Before applying the finish, clean up the joints with a needle file to remove any burrs and traces of glue.

50 Now for the difficult part: the second candlestick is made as similar to the first as possible. After it has been made, place the two together upside down to check that they are the same height. In this case the base thickness was adjusted.

FINISHING

51 At this stage I usually apply a couple of coats of satin finish lacquer. I do not use sanding sealer, as it has a habit of allowing the colour of the dark wood to run into the white wood. Once the lacquer has hardened, after about four hours, remount the candlestick between centres and sand using an abrasive pad to de-nib the wood. Go over the candlestick again with the needle file to remove any fine whiskers between the segments. The base is lacquered and the candlestick given a couple more coats of lacquer. De-nib the candlestick between coats with an abrasive pad.

52 The finished candlesticks should look something like this.

OFFSET CORIAN BOWL

Asymmetrical objects are more pleasing to the eye than symmetrical objects. But this isn't easy on a lathe. Instead of making one bowl, why not make two bowls from one cube of Corian? Then cut the resulting cube diagonally. These offset bowls make ideal presents and are perfect for serving olives. They are washable and food-safe.

Skill level:
● **Advanced**

OFFSET CORIAN BOWL

YOU WILL NEED:

EQUIPMENT
Circular saw
Lathe
Bandsaw
Disc sander

MATERIALS
8 black and 8 white Corian squares
measuring 8 x ½in (20cm x13mm)
CA glue
Corian base adhesive

TOOLS
Tungsten-tipped shear scraper
Half-round negative-rake scraper
Teardrop scraper
Callipers
Skew chisel
Parting tool

DESIGN

The way to make this offset bowl
is to construct a composite cube
by gluing squares of Corian sheet
together in layers. The cube is then
cut diagonally (see diagram) to
provide two offset bowls.

The centres are cut out before
construction. The inner and outer
diameters are drawn on one side
of the cube to show how much
Corian can be cut away before
gluing-up; it is easier to cut away
the waste beforehand than have
large amounts to turn away on
the lathe. The design shown in the
diagram can be easily varied to suit
the Corian offcuts available.

Block diagram

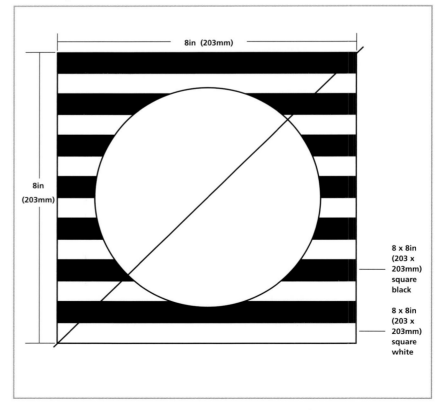

8in (203mm)

8in (203mm)

8 x 8in (203 x 203mm) square black

8 x 8in (203 x 203mm) square white

CUTTING AND CONSTRUCTION

1 First cut the Corian sheet into squares on the circular saw fitted with a laminate tungsten-tipped fine-tooth blade.

2 Assemble the cube dry and mark the inner and outer diameters using a pencil mounted in a compass.

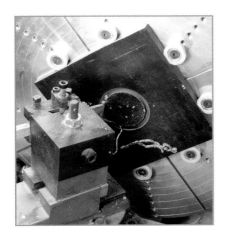

3 Mount the squares on the lathe using large button jaws – the four-button jaws work as equally well on round objects as square objects. I prefer to use a metalwork lathe to cut the inside of the rings using a parting-off tool, but they can be cut to size on a wood lathe using a thin parting tool. Position a square of ¼in (5mm) hardboard behind the Corian to avoid the parting tool hitting the jaws.

4 To get close to the inner diameter for turning later, cut some of the levels at an angle, as necessary.

5 The inner diameter of the layers is individually cut from the squares, starting at the smaller diameters and working up.

6 Make a jig from MDF to keep the composite square while gluing up. While thick CA glue works very well, I prefer to use Corian's own glue which is a colour-coordinated epoxy resin that cannot be seen after gluing up.

TIP: Corian is highly polished and to give the glue a surface to bite to it is best to rub the surfaces with 120-grit sandpaper beforehand.

7 I sometimes use thin card spacers in each corner to ensure the levels remain flat and the glue is of a consistent thickness. Repeat the process for the remaining levels.

8 When the composite has been constructed, leave the cube for 24 hours, as the glue takes time to cure between the layers.

9 Alternatively, you can do as I do, which is to cut the cube in half slowly on the bandsaw after about four hours to enable air to get to the glue inside.

10 Before mounting on the lathe, cut away the corners and create a flat surface for mounting on the chuck.

11 I prefer to glue the Corian to a wooden faceplate using thick CA glue.

TURNING

12 Clean up the rough edges on the outside using a tungsten-tipped shear scraper. Finish is not important at this stage, so the lathe speed can be held at about 500rpm; at this speed the Corian splinters, enabling the size to be cut back quickly. A finishing cut will need a much slower speed to achieve those beautiful shavings and a smooth finish.

13 Do not bring the outside down to size at this stage, just even out the curve of the bowl to leave the maximum thickness to support the turning of the inside.

14 Clean up the rim to accept an MDF disc to be used as a support in the lathe steady.

15 Turn the MDF rim smooth for the three-point steady. Mount the steady and cut out the inside of the MDF disc. Rough out the inside to size using a tungsten-tipped shear scraper.

16 Remove the central pip using a half-round negative-rake scraper.

17 Once the final size is approached reduce the lathe speed to give a smoother cut. Check the thickness all down the sides using callipers, then achieve the final finish using a teardrop scraper.

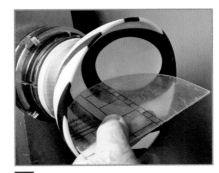

18 It is easier to work with a semi-circular template to obtain the correct inside shape of the bowl, otherwise the pattern may distort.

19 Remove the MDF ring and clean up the rim.

20 Now reverse the bowl on the lathe to finish the outside. A cone made from MDF acts as a very good support for the rim as a jam chuck. Start by using the tungsten-tipped scraper at a slow, 200rpm, speed to clean up the outside.

21 Check the bowl thickness using callipers, trying to achieve about ⅛in (3mm), then clean up surface marks on the sides using the negative-rake scraper. Before the bowl is parted off, sand and polish the inside with Mirka Abranet pads, starting at 120 grit and working up to 1000. You may have to keep going back to earlier grits to eliminate all the surface scratches. Remember, there is no gloss finish: the finish is the sanded material.

22 When the inside has been polished, buff it with a sheepskin mop using a car polish.

23 The inside should now shine with no visible scratches. Part off the bowl from the faceplate, cutting the final pip with a small saw.

FINISHING

24 Reverse the bowl on the lathe using a small wooden cone to support the inside on the headstock and a small steb centre on the tailstock. Bring the base down to size using the tungsten-tipped tool.

25 Clean up the base using a skew chisel on its side in shear-scraping mode, then re-check the sides for flatness and make any adjustments. Sand the sides as for the inside and polish the bowl as before.

26 Sand the base and the finished bowl should look something like this.

GLOSSARY

Aliphatic resin glue A yellow glue, ideal for gluing end-grain.

Air dried A technique of drying and seasoning wood using natural circulating air. A slow process – normally accepted to require one year for 1in (2.5cm) of thickness.

Backplate A means of supporting a piece of wood on the tailstock.

Bevel The ground surface on the end of the woodturning tool. The bevel usually rubs against the work and supports the edge.

Bowl gouge A general-purpose tool used for hollowing wooden bowls. It has a stronger shank than a spindle gouge to support its extension over the tool-rest when cutting deeply into bowls.

Burr The raised saw tooth-like edge on the woodworking tool raised after grinding. Sometimes honed off gouges but normally used very effectively on scrapers.

CA glue (Cyanoacrylate glue) Exceptionally quick-setting glue. Can be brittle; a flexible version is available with rubber content. Ideal for Plexiglas and Corian.

Chuck A clamping device to securely hold a piece of wood on the lathe for turning. Normally they have four self-centering jaws for woodturning; three for metal turning.

Epoxy resin glue A two-part glue used for boat building and gluing plastics such as Corian.

Faceplate A means of attaching a piece of wood to the lathe headstock. They can be made from steel or from wood.

Gouge A chisel with a curved body.

Grain The texture colour and pattern created by the growth of wood. Grain fibres are like a collection of drinking straws. The ends of the straws would be end-grain and the length of the straws would be side grain. Grain is usually tapered as the tree is itself tapered. 'With-the-grain' refers to slices up the taper of the tree. 'Against-the-grain' refers to slices from down the taper of the tree.

Green wood Freshly felled unseasoned timber with a high moisture content – 20%+.

Headstock The driven-end of the lathe.

Hollowing tool A special tool designed for hollowing out hollow-forms. It has a cut limiter and is ideal for roughing cuts for the inside of segmented bowls.

Jam chuck A means of holding a wooden object on the lathe by jamming it against a tapered driven wooden block – not a mechanical chuck.

Kiln dried A means of drying and seasoning wood quickly in a drying kiln. Usually to 15%.

Lathe A means of rotating a wooden object to be machined round. Originated as foot-operated pole lathes to today's variable speed electrically powered lathes.

Lathe steady A device for supporting delicate spindles and bowls from excessive vibration when turning.

Negative rake scraping A scraping technique using only the burr of the scraper. A conventional scraper with a 20–30° grind on its top edge is used. It eliminates any dig-in and is ideal on plastics and Corian.

Parting tool A thin-bladed straight-edged tool used for cutting a finished object from its holding base – parting off.

PU glue (Polyurethane wood glue) A strong wood glue. Needs clamping as it foams in humid air.

PVA glue (Polyvinyl Acetate glue) A good general-purpose wood glue. Not suitable for end-grain or plastics.

Scraper A flat tool used for shear scraping with a steep cutting edge – normally 80°. The tear-drop scraper has a 90° angle.

Shear scraping A safe and delicate method of scraping timber. The scraper or gouge is set at an angle of 45° to the tool rest – the cut is down the edge of the sloping tool. Used for segmented turning.

Tailstock The supporting end of the lathe.

Tungsten-tipped tool Tool designed to make use of Tungsten-Carbide tip's. The tips can be either brazed onto the shank or screwed on, which allows them to be interchanged when they become blunt.

CONVERSION CHART

Imperial to metric						Metric to imperial	
Inches (fractions)	Inches (decimal)	Millimetres	Inches (fractions)	Inches (decimal)	Millimetres	Millimetres	Inches
1/64	0.0156	0.3969	33/64	0.5156	13.0969	1	0.0394
1/32	0.0313	0.7938	17/32	0.5313	13.4938	1.5	0.0591
3/64	0.0469	1.1906	35/64	0.5469	13.8906	2	0.0787
1/16	0.0625	1.5875	9/16	0.5625	14.2875	2.5	0.0984
5/64	0.0781	1.9844	37/64	0.5781	14.6844	3	0.1181
3/32	0.0938	2.3813	19/32	0.5938	15.0813	3.5	0.1378
7/64	0.1094	2.7781	39/64	0.6094	15.4781	4	0.1575
1/8	0.1250	3.1750	5/8	0.6250	15.8750	4.5	0.1772
9/64	0.1406	3.5719	41/64	0.6406	16.2719	5	0.1969
5/32	0.1563	3.9688	21/32	0.6563	16.6688	5.5	0.2165
11/64	0.1719	4.3656	43/64	0.6719	17.0656	6	0.2362
3/16	0.1875	4.7625	11/16	0.6875	17.4625	6.5	0.2559
13/64	0.2031	5.1594	45/64	0.7031	17.8594	7	0.2756
7/32	0.2188	5.5563	23/32	0.7188	18.2563	7.5	0.2953
15/64	0.2344	5.9531	47/64	0.7344	18.6531	8	0.3150
1/4	0.2500	6.3500	3/4	0.7500	19.0500	8.5	0.3346
17/64	0.2656	6.7469	49/64	0.7656	19.4469	9	0.3543
7/32	0.2813	7.1438	25/32	0.7813	19.8438	9.5	0.3740
19/64	0.2969	7.5406	51/64	0.7969	20.2406	10	0.3937
5/16	0.3125	7.9375	13/16	0.8125	20.6375	10.5	0.4134
21/64	0.3281	8.3344	53/64	0.8281	21.0344	11	0.4331
11/32	0.3438	8.7313	27/32	0.8438	21.4313	11.5	0.4528
23/64	0.3594	9.1281	55/64	0.8594	21.8281	12	0.4724
3/8	0.3750	9.5250	7/8	0.8750	22.2250	12.5	0.4921
25/64	0.3906	9.9219	57/64	0.8906	22.6219	13	0.5118
13/32	0.4063	10.3188	29/32	0.9063	23.0188	13.5	0.5315
27/64	0.4219	10.7156	59/64	0.9219	23.4156	14	0.5512
7/16	0.4375	11.1125	15/16	0.9375	23.8125	14.5	0.5709
29/64	0.4531	11.5094	61/64	0.9531	24.2094	15	0.5906
15/32	0.4688	11.9063	31/32	0.9688	24.6063	15.5	0.6102
31/64	0.4844	12.3031	63/64	0.9844	25.0031	16	0.6299
1/2	0.5000	12.7000	1	1.0000	25.4000	16.5	0.6496

SUPPLIERS

UK

Ashley Isles (Edge Tools) Ltd
Tel: +44 (0)1790 763372
www.ashleyisles.co.uk
Manufacturers of fine turning tools.

Axminster Tool Centre
Tel: +44 (0)1297 33666
www.axminster.co.uk
Complete range of woodturning equipment,
tools and materials.

Felder UK Ltd
Tel: +44 (0)1908 635000
www.ukfelder.co.uk
Manufacturers of Hammer and Felder
woodworking machinery.

Isaac Lord
Tel: +44 (0)1494 835 200
www.isaaclord.co.uk
Extensive range of ironmongery, hardware,
woodworking machinery and materials.

Phil Irons Woodturning
Tel: +44 (0)1789 204052
www.philirons.co.uk
Suppliers of Vicmarc lathes and Woodcut Hollowing Tools

The Toolpost
Tel: +44 (0)1235 511101
www.toolpost.co.uk
Suppliers of woodworking tools, glues and finishes.

USA

Bill Smith
www.smithart.us
Open-segmented turning, Index Wheel templates.

Craft Supplies
Tel: +1 801 373 0917
www.woodturnerscatalog.com
Suppliers of woodturning equipment, tools and materials.

Curt Theobald
Tel: +01 307-245-3310
www.curttheobald.com
Supplier of wood art, segmenting DVDs and tutor.

Malcolm Tibbetts
Tel: +01 530-541-6135
www.tahoturner.com
Supplier of wood art, segmenting DVDs and tutor.

Woodturner Pro, LCC
www.woodturnerpro.com
Developers of Woodturner Pro, 3D DesignPro and Laminate
Pro, as used in the projects.

AUSTRALIA

Vicmarc Machinery PTY Ltd
Tel: +61 (07) 3284 3103
www.vicmarc.com
Manufacturers of woodturning lathes and equipment.

Further Reading

Audsley, G. & Audsley, B., *The Art of Polychromatic and Decorative Turning*, George Allen & Company, London, 1911

Brown, E. & Brown, C., *Polychromatic Assembly for Woodturning*, Linden Publishing Co, California, 1982

Hampton, R. E., *Segmented Turning – A Complete Guide*, Guild of Master Craftsmen Publications Ltd, Lewes, 2003

Kandler, B., *Segmented Turning – A Good Start*, Verified Software Products Co., California, 2004

Nish, D., *Woodturning with Ray Allen*, Fox Chapel Publishing, Pennsylvania, 2004

Pinto, E. & Pinto E., *Tunbridge and Scottish Souvenir Woodware*, G. Bell & Sons, London, 1970

Smith, B., *Segmented Wood Turning*, Schiffer Publishing Ltd, Pennsylvania, 2002

Tibbetts, M., *The Art of Segmented Woodturning*, Linden Publishing Inc., California, 2006

USEFUL WEBSITES

American Association of Woodturners (AAW)
www.woodturner.org
Parent body of woodturners in the USA and organisers of the annual Symposium.

Association of Segmented Woodturners – A Chapter of the AAW
www.segmentedwoodturners.org
The representative body of Segmenters around the world and organizers of the biannual Segmenting Symposium.

Association of Wood Turners of Great Britain (AWGB)
www.woodturners.co.uk
Parent body for UK woodturners and organisers of the biannual Woodturning Seminar.

Society of Ornamental Turners
www.the-sot.com
Representing ornamental tuners from around the world.

Woodworkers Institute
www.woodworkersinstitute.com
Forum for woodturners and reviews of *Woodturning Magazine*.

Worshipful Company of Turners
www.turnersco.com
The Turners Livery Company was granted a Royal Charter in 1604; previously the Guild of Turners established in 1295.

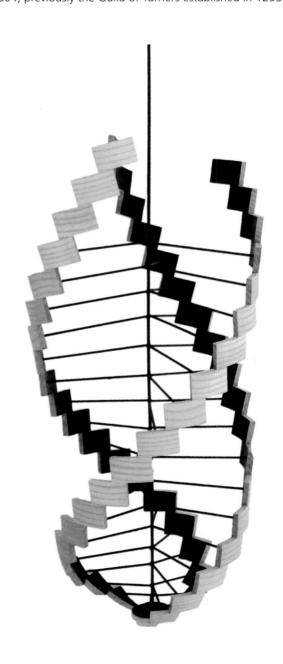

ABOUT THE AUTHOR

Dennis Keeling is a keen hobby turner, who has demonstrated segmented turning to Woodturning Clubs in the UK and in America. He started turning when he was just nine years old. Using a simple lathe attachment to his father's electric drill, he turned spindles from cut up broom stays. Unfortunately secondary school education did not cover woodturning and he went on to become an Industrial Engineer and later an IT specialist. Years later his wife reintroduced him to woodturning when she bought him a lathe for Christmas 1995.

He quickly became fascinated by the potential of segmenting, as it had no boundaries. He was soon turning Ali-Baba urns, large wine glass shapes, a variety of unusual tubs and other designs. He has gone on to win many prizes for his work at the Worshipful Company of Turners of London competitions; the Alexandra Palace competitions in London; and the Woodex competitions in Warwickshire.

He started writing articles for Woodturning magazine in 2003, which steered him into experimenting with other forms of segmenting and laminating, not only with Corian but also with Plexiglass (Perspex) and acrylics.

Dennis is a Director of the Segmented Woodturners Association, a Chapter of the American Association of Woodturners of which he is also a member. He is a member of the Middlesex Woodturners Association and in turn a member of the Association of Wood Turners in Great Britain. He is a Freeman of the Worshipful Company of Turners and a Freeman of the City of London. He is a member of the Society of Ornamental Turners.

ACKNOWLEDGEMENTS

I would like to thank the family of Ray Allen for allowing me to publish photographs of his work.

I would also like to thank Malcolm Tibbetts, Charles Faucher, Bud Latven, Curt Theobald, Bill Smith and Jerry Bennett for their help with the book and supplying photographs of their work.

Lastly, I would like to thank Mark Baker for his help and support in bringing together a cohesive book.

PICTURE CREDITS

Photos by **Dennis Keeling**, except for the following:

Anthony Bailey/GMC Publications, 2, 5, 40, 64 top, 65 right, 67 top right, 69 top left and right, middle left, 77 bottom left and right, 78, 80, 81, 82, 89 bottom, 90, 91, 92, 99 bottom, 100, 101, 102, 109 bottom, 110, 111, 112, 117 bottom, 118, 119, 120, 125 bottom, 126, 127, 128, 135 bottom, 136, 137, 138, 145, 146, 147, 148, 153 bottom, 154, 155, 156, 165 bottom, 166, 167, 168, 173 bottom.
Bill Smith, p.14, p.31 top.
Bud Latven, p.12 bottom left and right.
Charles Faucher, p.42.
Curt Theobald, p.15.
Jerry Bennett, p.16.
Malcolm Tibbetts, p.10 top and bottom left, p.13.
Ray Allen family, p.12 top left and right.

Illustrations by **Rob Janes** except for the following, by **Dennis Keeling**: 42, 82, 92, 102, 112, 128, 138, 148, 156.

INDEX

To place an order or to request a catalogue, contact:

GMC Publications Ltd.

Castle Place, 166 High Street, Lewes, East Sussex, BN7 1XU, United Kingdom

Tel: +44 (0)1273 488005   Fax: +44 (0)1273 402866   www.gmcbooks.com